D1624519

Phyllis Segal

Words of Praise for
The New Golden Rules
꧁꧂

"**The New Golden Rules** is filled with wonderful messages of healing, love, and light. Dr. Dharma has an engaging and uplifting style of teaching about the important connection between spirituality and our health. He speaks from the voice of love and experience. I found the book to be very heart-opening."
— **Doreen Virtue, Ph.D.**, the author of *Angel Medicine* and *Healing with the Angels*

"Powerful! Honest! Timely! In **The New Golden Rules**, Dr. Dharma Singh Khalsa offers a rich collection of his life lessons that invites us into a deeper journey of our own. Along the way, we discover the practical spirituality that is the hallmark of true wisdom. This book is an essential addition to the library of anyone on the 'Path.'"
— **Gregg Braden**, the author of *The God Code* and *The Isaiah Effect*

"**The New Golden Rules** is perfect for anyone ready to take the next step in their spiritual growth toward inner peace and joy."
— **Joan Z. Borysenko, Ph.D.**, the author of *Inner Peace for Busy People* and *Inner Peace for Busy Women*

"This is a warm, beautiful spiritual journey, and a real testament on how to live life."
— **James Van Praagh**, spiritual medium

"A beautiful and wonderful book of golden rules for the spirit to love your life by. A must read for anyone who wants to take the next step in their spiritual growth."
— **Judith Orloff, M.D.**, the author of *Positive Energy* and *Second Sight*

"**The New Golden Rules** is a wonderful book that provides the spiritual wisdom and guidance we all need, now more than ever."
— **Cheryl Richardson**, the author of *Stand Up for Your Life* and *Life Makeovers*

"Magnificent! *The New Golden Rules* is a book whose time
has come. This book is a reservoir of wisdom and spiritual
warmth for the soul. It's a wonderful treasure."
— **Caroline Myss**, the author of
Anatomy of the Spirit and *Invisible Acts of Power*

"*The New Golden Rules* provide an indispensable common
ground for people of every belief system. As we accelerate
through globalization and technological development, it is
critical that we remain primarily focused on ethics, goodness,
and solidarity. Dharma has provided us, in an enjoyably
written format, with the framework for this common beneficent
focus. I will keep my copy on my desktop."
— **Martine Rothblatt, Ph.D.**, chairperson/CEO of United
Therapeutics Corporation; medical ethicist, and the author of
Your Life or Mine and *Unzipped Genes*

"*In an era when the only viable and sustainable way to
change our world is through a change in consciousness, not
politics, this book offers a simple and practical guide. It is based
on scientifically accurate as well as spiritually sound principles.
These are clearly enunciated through the healing power of transformative stories and practical meditation exercises.*"
— **Victor S. Sierpina**, M.D., Associate Professor of Family Medicine,
University of Texas Medical Branch

"'Heaven on earth is that condition of living where you feel love
all around you and see God in all.' These words from Dr.
Dharma Sing Khalsa's book *The New Golden Rules* speak to
a universal human desire to experience deep spirituality. He
writes with simplicity, sincerity, and succinctness. His message
transcends religious boundaries and cultural barriers. If everyone adopts these basic principles, as he says, 'Our love can
change the planet.' Read this book! It will change your world!"
— **Michelle Sierpina**, M.S., Founding Director, Academy for Lifelong
Learning, University of Texas Medical Branch

"*First Class! Dharma's writing is very penetrating.*"
— **Yogi Bhajan, Ph.D.**, master of Kundalini and White Tantric Yoga

The New Golden Rules

Also by Dharma Singh Khalsa, M.D.

Books

Brain Longevity (Warner Books, 1997)
The Pain Cure (Warner Books, 1999)
Meditation as Medicine (Pocket Books—Simon & Schuster, 2001)
Food as Medicine (Atria Books—Simon & Schuster, 2003)

Kit

The Better Memory Kit (Hay House, 2004)

CDs

(A series of 7 CDs with Spirit Voyage Music)

First Chakra: Morning Call

Second Chakra Meditation

Meditations for the Third and Fifth Chakras

Fourth Chakra: Meditation for a Calm Heart

Sixth Chakra Meditation

Seventh and Eighth Chakras: Meditation to Heal Self and Others

Wake Up to Wellness

Love is In You, by Dr. Khalsa's group, Bliss, featuring Dr. D
and Master L (presents a unique combination of pop/rock
melodies and inspiring words)
Created to uplift and enlighten (© 2004 drdharma Music)

Audiocassettes

Meditation for Healing: A Dialogue Between Dharma Singh
Khalsa, M.D., and Deepak Chopra, M.D. (Hay House, 2003).

Please visit Hay House USA: **www.hayhouse.com**
Hay House Australia: **www.hayhouse.com.au**
Hay House UK: **www.hayhouse.co.uk**
Hay House South Africa: **orders@psdprom.co.za**

The New Golden Rules

An
Essential
Guide
to
Spiritual
Bliss

Dharma Singh Khalsa, M.D.

HAY HOUSE, INC.
Carlsbad, California
London • Sydney • Johannesburg
Vancouver • Hong Kong

Copyright © 2005 by Dharma Singh Khalsa

Published and distributed in the United States by: Hay House, Inc., P.O. Box 5100, Carlsbad, CA 92018-5100 • *Phone:* (760) 431-7695 or (800) 654-5126 • *Fax:* (760) 431-6948 or (800) 650-5115 • www.hayhouse.com • *Published and distributed in Australia by:* Hay House Australia Pty. Ltd., 18/36 Ralph St., Alexandria NSW 2015 • *Phone:* 612-9669-4299 • *Fax:* 612-9669-4144 • www.hayhouse.com.au • *Published and distributed in the United Kingdom by:* Hay House UK, Ltd. • Unit 62, Canalot Studios • 222 Kensal Rd., London W10 5BN • *Phone:* 44-20-8962-1230 • *Fax:* 44-20-8962-1239 • www.hayhouse.co.uk • *Published and distributed in the Republic of South Africa by:* Hay House SA (Pty), Ltd., P.O. Box 990, Witkoppen 2068 • *Phone/Fax:* 27-11-706-6612 • orders@psdprom.co.za • *Distributed in Canada by:* Raincoast • 9050 Shaughnessy St., Vancouver, B.C. V6P 6E5 • *Phone:* (604) 323-7100 • *Fax:* (604) 323-2600

Editorial supervision: Jill Kramer • *Design:* Jenny Richards
Illustrations by: Siri Kartar Kaur Khalsa

All rights reserved. No part of this book may be reproduced by any mechanical, photographic, or electronic process, or in the form of a phonographic recording; nor may it be stored in a retrieval system, transmitted, or otherwise be copied for public or private use—other than for "fair use" as brief quotations embodied in articles and reviews without prior written permission of the publisher.

The author of this book does not dispense medical advice or prescribe the use of any technique as a form of treatment for physical or medical problems without the advice of a physician, either directly or indirectly. The intent of the author is only to offer information of a general nature to help you in your quest for emotional and spiritual well-being. In the event you use any of the information in this book for yourself, which is your constitutional right, the author and the publisher assume no responsibility for your actions.

Library of Congress Cataloging-in-Publication Data

Singh Khalsa, Dharma.
  The new golden rules : an essential guide to spiritual bliss / Dharma Singh Khalsa.
    p. cm.
  ISBN 1-4019-0466-1 (hardcover)
  1. Spiritual life. I. Title.
  BL624.S57 2005
  204'.4—dc22

                                    2004025208

                        ISBN 13: 978-1-4019-0466-1
                           ISBN 10: 1-4019-0466-1

                    08   07   06   05   4   3   2   1
                        1st printing, March 2005

                 Printed in the United States of America

For His Holiness the Siri Singh Sahib, Yogi Bhajan

Contents

Introduction: We Are One xi

Chapter 1: My One Prayer 1

Chapter 2: Heaven on Earth 3

Chapter 3: Do Unto Others 19

Chapter 4: The First New Golden Rule:
Discover Your Miracle 33

    • *Part I:* Energize Your Spirit 37

    • *Part II:* Satisfy Your Soul......................49

    • *Part III:* Enjoy the Company
of the Holy 60

Chapter 5: The Second New Golden Rule:
Listen and Agree 71

Chapter 6: The Third New Golden Rule:
Dissolve Your Blocks 89

Chapter 7: The Fourth New Golden Rule:
See the Other Person As Yourself 121

Afterword: In God I Dwell 137

Acknowledgments 147

About the Author 149

Resources 151

INTRODUCTION

We Are One

I'm a lot like you. Oh yes, I know that I have an exotic-sounding name, wear a turban, and sport a long beard. But even considering that, you and I are quite similar: We're both human beings, and more important, we're spiritual beings living on Earth at the same time—here to shine, and to discover our Divine inner nature. Before you begin your exploration of the New Golden Rules, however, I'd like to share a bit of my own journey with you.

I was born in Cleveland, Ohio, in 1946. When I was very young, perhaps four or five, I developed a serious illness, and my doctor thought that it would be best for my recovery and long-term health if my family moved to the sunshine state of Florida. My parents had just divorced, so on my sixth birthday, my mother took me to live in Miami Beach, where her younger brother (a doctor) and his family also lived.

Growing up there was nice—I went to the beach, played sports every afternoon in the park, and of course, attended school. After high school, I entered the premed program at the University of Florida, returning home during the summers, during which time I enjoyed working at a couple of different hospitals.

Upon completing college, I was fortunate enough to be accepted at the Creighton University School of Medicine in Omaha, Nebraska. It was cold there for a Florida boy, but the inclement weather gave me plenty of time to study. In fact, that's about *all* I did.

Following medical school, I decided to become an anesthesiologist and was accepted at the University of California, San Francisco (UCSF), which was considered by many to be the top anesthesia program in the world. (That is, unless you were at Harvard, which considered itself number one and UCSF second place, but we knew the truth.)

During my internship (the first year after medical school), I took a course in Transcendental Meditation (TM). My professional program was difficult, especially since I was continually going to the parties held by my peers and colleagues. As this way of life took its toll on me, I figured that I needed to try a different approach to living—one that gave me extra energy along with a relaxed state of mind—and I found that meditation did just what I wanted. I also thought that if it was good enough for the Beatles (who, as you may recall, studied TM), it was good enough for me, so off I went to learn my secret mantra.

Meditating helped me by giving me more stamina to get through those long, stressful nights on call, and encouraged me to become more creative. It turned out that I needed to develop that creative energy because after my first year of residency (my second year post-medical school), I was elected chief resident in anesthesiology at UCSF. That was quite an honor.

My new position meant doing research, so I became immersed in two projects. One involved developing the best anesthetic approach to a special kind of open-heart surgery, and we found that the winning technique was the one that lowered the patient's stress the most. You may think that's a no-brainer, but in the mid-'70s, it was actually quite an innovative concept. The results from this work turned into my first scientific paper.

My second research project involved the field of obstetrics. I was part of the team that discovered that an epidural is the safest and most effective childbirth-anesthetic technique for both mother and child, especially during a caesarean section. In those days, you could find me running to the operating room (OR) in the middle of the night, placing epidurals and then drawing the mother's blood to measure her endorphin levels. Endorphins, as you probably know, are the body's own version of morphine. Their presence determines the amount of stress in the body, and we found that our procedure reduced stress dramatically.

Based on this research, the epidural became a very important tool in helping women have safe and pleasant childbirth experiences. Even now, when I share this story during a presentation I'm giving, a woman or two in the audience will raise their hand and say, "Oh, thank you!" Being involved in this obstetrical anesthesia research was one of the most rewarding parts of my professional medical experience.

After my training at UCSF was complete, I moved to Albuquerque, New Mexico. I'd visited a friend there a few years before and had fallen in love with the place. It wasn't a totally logical move, however, because I was a highly trained super-specialist who was on track to become a professor of obstetrical anesthesiology at one of the world's foremost medical centers—and now I was moving to a small Southwestern town. But I felt a tremendous power pulling me to New Mexico, and I couldn't resist that force, so I went along with it and landed a job at a sleepy little medical center in the high desert.

It wasn't long after I arrived that I made an important decision: I decided that I wanted to take a yoga class. During medical school, I'd read a book called *28 Days to Yoga* (now available as *Richard Hittleman's Yoga 28 Day Exercise Plan*) and had followed the stretching exercises in it. During my days in San Francisco, I practiced a little yoga from another book, and as I mentioned, took the TM training program. Those experiences had a lasting positive effect on me, so I wanted to take a real class. One day I asked Leslie, the wife of my friend John, if she knew where I could attend a session. She opened up a little alternative newspaper called the *Albuquerque Alibi*, pointed to an advertisement, and said, "I heard that's a good one." So off I went, never anticipating how my life was about to be completely transformed.

The class took place in a little house called an "ashram" in the university district. I went in and sat down on the comfortable green carpet as a tall young man with a long red beard and a white turban came into the room. He sat down, raised both his arms above his head, and started breathing very fast through his nose. He then asked the other five members of the class to join in, and we did. I was immediately transported to a place I'd only dreamed about . . . a timeless, inspiring, and healing spot. I felt absolutely fantastic as I thought, *This is for me.*

For the next two years, I was a regular student of this powerful practice, which is called *kundalini yoga* and includes special meditation techniques. I learned that it had recently been brought to the United States by an Indian yoga master named Yogi Bhajan, whom I'll talk about throughout this book.

Finally, after taking classes and studying kundalini yoga and meditation for two years, I had the opportunity to meet this influential leader. During Thanksgiving weekend in 1981, I traveled up to Española, a small hamlet about an hour and a half north of Albuquerque, to attend an advanced workshop called White Tantric Yoga (which I'll discuss later on as well). What I want you to know now is that I had an incredibly powerful spiritual experience that weekend.

During a break between exercises, I went up to the front of the auditorium to meet Yogi Bhajan. It was the first time I'd done this type of yoga or donned a white turban. As I approached the stage where the master was sitting, for some reason I started thinking about my uncle in Florida—the one I mentioned earlier who'd been a doctor. He'd died at 63, a young age to pass away, and I'd always wondered if he was spiritually at peace.

Yogi Bhajan looked at me with his luminescent dark eyes, and I felt as if he were reading my soul. But he wasn't—instead, he was reading my mind. "Do you think you can go before the public like that?" he asked, referring to my wearing a turban.

"It might take some time," I replied.

"Time? What's time?" he answered. "Do you think 63 years is a long time?"

When he uttered that specific number, I realized that he somehow knew I was thinking about my uncle. At that point, I decided that I wanted to get a spiritual name, which would be nothing more than an indicator of my potential. It would signify my highest promise as a human being—but it would also be my choice to try to follow the path that would let me live up to its meaning.

To initiate the process, I wrote down my birth date and handed it to the yogi. He then performed a numerological calculation to determine my spiritual name, in addition to his own highly developed intuition and ability to read human auras.

As he handed me the paper and I saw my spiritual name in his own handwriting, my life unfolded before my eyes. I didn't have a past-life or near-death experience. The only way I can describe it to you is as a *future-life* experience; in other words, I had a vision of my destiny.

As I read my new name, Dharma Singh Khalsa (which means "a pure lion on a victorious path"), I realized that I no longer had to use powerful anesthetic drugs to put people to sleep. Right then and there, I knew that I was destined to teach others how to wake up spiritually and heal in their bodies, minds, and souls. In that one moment of understanding, my life changed and I became Dr. Dharma.

After that weekend, I had to go back to work at the hospital. I told the chairman of my department that, beginning in two days, I'd be wearing a turban, and I repeated my intention the next day, telling him that the change would occur the following morning. Sure enough, when Wednesday arrived, I went to work wearing a turban, and I've worn one ever since.

This practice signifies that I'm an advanced student of

Yogi Bhajan's, and a Sikh. Sikhism is the fifth largest religion in the world. Even though it originated in India, it's a separate, independent doctrine not affiliated with either Hinduism or Islam. This monotheistic faith is rooted in the belief in one true immortal essence of reality that is the doer of everything and part of every person; its other basic tenet is that life is to be lived to the fullest as a spiritual being, and followers are expected to help others. Of course, it's possible to still be a spiritual seeker and a student of yoga without wearing a turban, but I felt so strongly about my new path in life that I wanted to go all the way.

Over the next ten years, I experienced a lot of personal and professional change as I went from being a practicing clinical anesthesiologist to a holistic pain physician to an integrative-medicine specialist working to help patients prevent and reverse memory loss. Since then, I've become an author, with six books under my belt (including this one), as well as the creator of a number of meditation CDs and a fun pop-music album entitled *Love Is in You* with my group, Bliss.

Quite often I'm asked how I've made these changes, and I answer, "Evolution." Over time, I've evolved to a higher level of existence by following the same steps that I'll share with you in the following chapters. In essence, I've become myself—only better—and you can do this, too. But don't worry—your transformation doesn't have to be as dramatic as mine. Everyone's path is unique.

—⌒⌒—

Change, I've learned, happens slowly, even if it sometimes appears to be frighteningly fast. I didn't start wearing a turban on Wednesday and become enlightened on

Thursday, despite the flash of insight I'd had the preceding weekend. Very few people can become one with their Higher Power overnight. It just doesn't happen that way. Instead, as with most things in life worth pursuing, a plan is required in order to be successful. I've done a lot of work to realize my spiritual nature, and I've put that experience into this book, giving you an essential and practical guide to achieving spiritual bliss.

We all have our own healing journey and spiritual path, and I've been walking mine since that wonderful day in 1981. This book, as I've mentioned, is a culmination of what I've learned along the way. It's not just philosophy, though—it's based on practical experience. Remember that I'm an anesthesiologist by training, and we're people of action who don't just sit around talking about what needs to happen. We figure out the best way to get the job done.

I'm going to outline four basic steps to help you move to the next level of living a spiritual lifestyle and realizing bliss. I'll talk more about all that soon, but for now I want to point out that I've written from a universal, nonreligious perspective. Of course, from time to time I'll quote a spiritual leader or scripture (for example, Buddha; the Bible; or my own teacher, Yogi Bhajan). I've included these ideas from enlightened beings and writings to help deepen your experience and give you a variety of perspectives on finding bliss. I hope that you'll assimilate all these ideas and distill from them what's most useful for your own journey.

I also share accounts of people who have walked down this road in what I call "Stories on the Path," which I believe you'll enjoy very much and find helpful, interesting, and inspiring. There are also little vignettes with the heading "The Master Speaks" that illustrate points that provide a high-level perspective on spiritual living. Finally, I'll give you a few simple, yet very effective, mind/body meditation exercises as practical tools to help you make the transformation I discuss in that particular chapter (such as releasing fear). You'll soon discover how different meditations have specific purposes.

In general, once you decide that an exercise resonates with you, it's best to practice it for 40 days in a row, making sure to fulfill the prescribed time each day (for example, 11 minutes). You may wonder, *What's the reason for this?* Well, according to advanced spiritual thought, it takes 40 days to ingrain a change in your being. (That's why 40 is such a profound spiritual number.)

We've been given the great gift of a body, mind, and soul; and in our Western way of thinking, we value perfection, as well as competition and being "number one." What I'd like you to discover through the exercises and ideas in this book is that you don't have to be perfect. Rather, the purpose of life is to live in peaceful balance, bringing harmony to all of your being and making you feel cozy. When you experience that, your values will change as your priorities shift from being perfect to appreciating serenity and joy. That is bliss.

We're all on a quest to realize our highest potential in this lifetime, and it's an exciting adventure. I salute you and congratulate you for taking this step—I know you'll never regret it.

In the first chapter, we'll begin with a prayer, using an easy breathing exercise to help you tune in to your Divine inner being and set your vibration to be in concert with the energy in this book. You're going to love it.

Peace to all. Life to all. Love to all.

CHAPTER ONE

My One Prayer

Please center yourself by taking a nice long, slow, deep breath through your nose. Calm your mind and realize that there's nowhere else to go and nothing else to do or figure out. All you have to do is just breathe.

As you do, go to the spot in your heart and soul where you'll find your one deepest prayer. Immerse yourself in that light now . . . feel it, be it, and enjoy it.

An example of a profound request might be: "My one prayer is that You grant me Your protection. My one prayer is that You guide me in my life. My one prayer is that I merge into Your light." What's your prayer? Discover it as you go within yourself.

Continue breathing deeply through your nose as you allow yourself to more clearly understand your one most important prayer, and then use your knowledge of it to focus in your mind's eye. Connect with your intention and your projection of it, and feel the love in your heart. Inhale again strongly through your nose, hold your breath, and then relax effortlessly as you surround yourself with your most sincere desire.

Now, please inhale fully, and go to your deepest wish with your mind's eye. Exhale your breath, then inhale and exhale again through your nose, and move out beyond yourself. Expand your energy in order to send your prayer to your family members and friends.

Please inhale again now, and hold your breath for the peace of the world, for the health of all, and to make everybody happy, so those who are lonely may find their partners, and so God may shower mercy upon every single person in the world.

Say your prayer on this inhalation, and then exhale. This process is the charity of the breath.

Inhale once again, and as you do, pray for all the dear related ones (known and unknown) on the whole planet—for those who are sick, unhappy, or need spirit. Send this thought out to them by praying on this breath . . . and then let the air go.

One more time, breathe in deeply and radiate a petition to end all causes and effects that cause women, children, and men to be unhappy or in pain.

Send a prayer to stop war and destruction.

Send a prayer to end hatred and jealousy.

Please finish by saying your own prayer on this final breath . . . and then let it go.

CHAPTER TWO

Heaven on Earth

Do you believe that God might talk to you? Have you ever had the experience of feeling the presence of a Higher Power guiding your life, or has God given you a message of direction in your dreams? If so, then you know that such things are possible. If you haven't experienced anything like this, do you believe that God really may come into your life?

Do you wonder if it's actually true that God gave Moses the Ten Commandments on Mount Sinai? Did He speak to the prophet Muhammad, and 700 years earlier give a message to Jesus, who fasted in the desert for 40 days, praying so deeply for a sign?

I believe that God has spoken with people throughout history, and that He does talk to us even today. How can I be so sure? Because I've had a few messages myself. Here are some of the things God has said to me:

"You've worked hard and done well. Now it's time to get serious."

"Make corrections."

"Meditate on Me, and help others do the same."

But the most profound message I ever received from God came to me in a dream while I was in India. One night while visiting friends, my wife and I slept in the bed normally occupied by their saintly three-and-a-half-year-old son, Hari Tehel (whose name means "God's messenger"). In my dream, a presence I can only describe as the one all-powerful Creator—God—directed me to write a very particular book. The dream presence told me that after I did so, I'd speak to thousands of people at a time. It was a startling, powerful, and transformational experience that led to the volume you're reading at this very moment.

What I didn't realize at the time of the dream was the road I'd have to travel to write this book. Fulfilling God's direction has been a long, wonderful journey, yet also quite challenging at times. I'll tell you about many aspects of my journey in the coming chapters, and share the healing and spiritual stories of others who are also walking on this path of spirit. It's my prayer that this will help you define your next step leading to the bright light of spiritual bliss.

Peace in Ourselves and Our World

All of our journeys are similar in many ways. We've all been evolving for many years—perhaps even from birth—and because of our joint evolution, we have a common ground: the spiritual spark within each of us that's there from the beginning of our lives until the moment that we take our last breath. To realize sacred joy in your life now, you must learn to light that fire of the Divine within yourself—and you'll discover how to do that in this book.

Perhaps you've been drawn to *The New Golden Rules* because you've reached a crossroads in your spiritual growth and development. You may have explored the beginning stages of transformation and realize that it's now time to move on to reach higher levels of spiritual maturity in your life. I know in my heart that the ideas I present to you will help you tremendously in taking the next step in your transition to living a deeper, richer, and more meaningful life.

Many of us are on a quest for inner peace because we so desperately want to stop the insanity of war. We've learned in school about the horror of the many wars our recent and remote ancestors fought and, unfortunately, we've had to witness and endure some of these events in our own lifetimes as well.

It's time to put an end to this. I believe we've had enough of war (I know *I* certainly have). I also see more and more individuals recognizing that world peace starts with our own *inner* peace. If we don't have love in our hearts, we'll never have peace in our world, because the larger picture is always a reflection of our collective selves. Every one of us needs and wants deep inner healing, tranquility, and balance in our lives and in the lives of our loved ones. We're longing to belong to a global family of higher values and consciousness.

Perhaps we've learned some of life's major (and at times, more painful) lessons at the hands of time. Now we're ready to use our personal experience to tune in to the positive energy that also exists in our world, hearts, and minds. For us to succeed in facilitating the transformation of the planet from one of constant war to one of harmony and peace, that power must become the major driving force in our lives. As the first prime minister of India, Jawaharal Nehru, said, "Peace is not merely the absence of war. It is also a state of mind. Lasting peace can only come to peaceful people."

Our combined efforts and prayers are working (and the New Golden Rules will help you increase your own contributions). Although war gets the headlines, peace is breaking out all over the world. Nongovernmental groups tracking armed conflict globally report a general decline in numbers of war casualties. There were 19 major armed conflicts in the world in 2003, a sharp drop from 33 wars in 1991, according to the authoritative Stockholm International Peace Research Institute.

Not only are the numbers of wars decreasing, but their intensity is as well—that is, the bloodshed in each conflict is declining. Because of the Iraq war, the number of deaths from hostilities rose to 20,000 in 2003 from 15,000 in 2002. But these figures are fewer than the 100,000 fatalities in the 1990s, and way down from the post–World War II peak of 700,000 in 1951.

This is not to say that we don't certainly still have a long way to go, because we do. So let's keep up our work to put an end to war, and project our intention of no more fighting or killing. Let our daily prayer be, in the words of the Old Testament: "To turn [our] swords into ploughshares and [our] spears into pruning hooks. Nation shall not lift up sword against nation. Neither shall they learn war anymore."

Heaven on Earth

I'm very humbled that the One Spirit has touched me and given me the opportunity to share the wisdom that I've gained on my journey through life. It's my blessing to be able to give you the same opportunity that I've had during my own spiritual transformation. I was touched by a master who made me pure, and just as he helped me discover my own real, Divine, immortal self, I'll help you discover your own true identity. In this way, we'll both be able to reach our full potential as spiritual beings in this lifetime, to know God and live in His light while we're still dwelling on Earth in these human forms. We'll enjoy Heaven on Earth in the here-and-now, and work together to spread peace and light throughout the world.

What do I mean by this? You've probably mentioned the phrase to yourself a time or two, perhaps while in your lover's arms, or on a beautiful beach in some exotic land watching the sunlight kiss the horizon.

To many spiritualists, this idea of Heaven on Earth has a number of ethereal, yet rather precise, meanings. It may have the connotation of being in a so-called state of liberation, where you feel free of the demands and cares of the world while still living in your body. In high yogic thought, this state of existence is called *jivan mukht,* or being in paradise while still being alive. That may sound confusing at first, but it's actually quite easy to understand. It simply means that you're deeply at peace, but you didn't have to die and go to Heaven to feel that way.

You see, Heaven on Earth is actually a concept for *living.* Its main principle is that life is a joy and should be lived as such. This bliss is achieved through the practice of meditation and by following certain actions (all of which I'll discuss in detail). Rather than living with the hope of finding happiness after death, you achieve it while you're still very much alive. That is, the hope of discovering something vague later is replaced by the experience of inner peace in the here-and-now, and in this way, you become fulfilled.

The famous Beatles guitarist George Harrison once said, "Everything else can wait but finding God and loving one another." Heaven on Earth is that condition of living where you feel love all around you and see God in all people and things. It's quite attainable, and although it may require a lot of good spiritual work to get there, the results sometimes manifest in seemingly unremarkable ways that make life much more worthwhile.

Here's a simple example of this happiness being expressed in a fairly ordinary way. One time I was chatting with Dr. Deepak Chopra, whose daughter had just had a baby. I was thinking of the possibility of my own children presenting me with a grandchild someday, and I was wondering who I'd find in the face of that infant: Would I see myself, the face of my children's mother, or the characteristics of a parent? With this in mind, I asked Deepak, "What do you see when you look at your granddaughter?"

As his eyes welled up, the eminent physician, mind/body pioneer, and spiritual teacher looked at me and said, "I see God."

I was instantly reminded that we all have the possibility of seeing God everywhere and feeling His love emanating from everyone. We simply need to have that intention and then allow it to manifest. That state of being is bliss, and that way of living is called "Heaven on Earth." In other words, we each have the power to create our own paradise.

Heaven on Earth and the Near-Death Experience

Modern medical science tells us that many people have found this true peace during what's become known as a near-death experience (NDE). As you may know, during an NDE a person suffers an accident, an illness, or another very serious malady, which is often considered fatal—at least for a time. During the period that they're considered "medically dead," they report floating above their body or being detached from the physical self in some way. To the amazement of the doctors and nurses who hear these stories, the patients may later report the exact details of their medical care (for example, being given life support of some kind).

Often, medical professionals are quite skeptical of NDEs. They don't believe that the experience could possibly be real, and consider it to be caused by some type of brain abnormality, perhaps a lack of oxygen or blood flow.

However, medical science is casting an interesting new light on this phenomenon. I discovered one scientific report of a female patient who'd apparently died. She reported that she'd floated lazily outside her body to the top floor of the hospital. When a physician said that he didn't believe her, she told him that she saw a yellow sneaker on the ledge of the roof of the hospital building. To that doctor's amazement (and the surprise of everyone else involved in the case), when the top of the building was explored, they found the yellow shoe. When asked by the startled crew to further describe her experience, she simply stated, "It was Heaven on Earth."

A profound fact about NDEs is that the people who've had them say that they felt no fear during that time, only peace, love, and happiness; and some have even reported experiencing true joy for the first time ever. Moreover, when they've returned to their physical bodies, they no longer have any fear at all of either life or death. Instead, they often say that they'll welcome death when it comes again, because the transition is what they call "going home."

Having an NDE is certainly eye-opening. What's so striking to many of those who've had one is that they gain so much clarity about themselves during the experience. They say that at the time, it's as if they're in a Divine space where their Higher Power (perhaps Jesus) or a bright light comes to them and instructs them in their true purpose or mission in life. In other words, their NDE teaches them why they were sent to Earth in the first place—why their soul chose to take a human birth.

The NDE is so enlightening—and so important—because it answers one of the key questions everyone asks at one time or another: "Who am I and why am I here? What is the meaning of my life?" A person may receive a life-altering answer to that profoundly personal question while undergoing this dramatic experience, and it's after they've been given this knowledge that they return to their physical body.

Although it may be quite a shock to return to their body (even a disappointment sometimes), many who've had this happen go about their life's work calmly once back on Earth, as if they were above it all. Yet they're very much alive and participating in the world, their family life, and their work with more attention to detail and more delight than they ever had before—and quite often more than they could have ever hoped to imagine.

Let me share a story with you that illustrates these ideas: Once when he was a young man, my spiritual teacher, His Holiness the Siri Singh Sahib, Yogi Bhajan, had a near-death experience. After a long trek in the Himalayas, he fell ill from dehydration, passed out, and was declared dead. By some miracle, after being gone for 45 minutes, he was revived. Later he recalled the vision he had while theoretically in the state of suspended animation. During his NDE, he came to a fork in a road where he was given two choices: On the right-hand side, there was a cozy tavern with friends and relatives asking him to enter. On the left, he saw quite a contrary image—a cold and snowy path.

At that moment, he realized that he was to choose neither, but should return to his body and live out his natural life in service to humanity. To the betterment of his hundreds of thousands of students and the many teachers he's trained, he came back to life. Based on his NDE, he gave the following sage advice: "When the time comes, choose the snowy path. It will lead to liberation from your karmas."

He also shared in his account of that experience that it isn't enough to just exist or pass through this short time on Earth that we call life. Rather, our purpose on this planet is to make the world a better place. We're here to serve, inspire, and uplift our fellow human beings.

A Story on the Path: Dana's Date with Destiny

This is the first of this book's Stories on the Path, in which I'll share the ways in which certain individuals have lived out the principles of this book.

I met Dana, a 26-year-old healer who's mature beyond her years, at a health spa where I was vacationing. As we struck up a conversation, I realized how important her experience was and how much knowledge she had to offer about her own spiritual transformation, which involved a near-death experience. So, here is Dana's date with destiny, as she told it to me:

Dr. D: You had a near-death experience that changed your life. What led up to it?

Dana: At age 13, my life was a painful struggle. There'd been a lot of abuse in my childhood, and a lot of pain. I was deep into my despair and feeling very, very sorry for myself. I took a bunch of my mother's sleeping pills, which I'd grown up seeing her abuse, and then I phoned my best friend to say good-bye. Although I didn't tell her what I'd done, she figured out that something was wrong and came rushing over to take me to the hospital. While the doctors were working on me, I died and left my body.

Dr. D: You were clinically dead?

Dana: I was declared clinically dead for more than a minute and a half in the hospital.

Dr. D: What do you remember about that?

Dana: I remember being above my body, almost like floating on the ceiling. I could see the doctors working on me, and I could see the other side of the room.

Dr. D: What were they doing when they were working on you?

Dana: They were trying to revive me—pumping my chest, trying to give me oxygen, just all kinds of stuff. Actually, I can't remember all that they were doing because I was kind of floating as I was looking at them, and just observing them from a very peaceful place. At the same time, I saw my mother and my best friend on the other side of the wall. My friend was crying, and my mother was scared and angry.

Dr. D: She was angry at you for dying?

Dana: She was *always* angry at me, but she didn't know at that point that I was dead because the doctors were still working on me. She was just furious out there; she was yelling, and I could see the whole process that she and my friend were going through.

I also had a view of my body—and the doctors, too—so I watched that for a while, and then I felt as if I were being pulled up into a light, like through a tunnel. Almost all that I remember from when I was in that space is that there were all these beings around me, and there was a lot of love. It was very warm, and they told me that I had to go back. I didn't want to leave them, but they convinced me at that point that I had a purpose in my life and needed to return.

Dr. D: Did they tell you what it was?

Dana: No, not that I remember. But the thing is that when I came back, it was with a great sense of purpose, and I had such strength and vision that every obstacle in my life was gone.

Dr. D: When you say that you had this sense of direction, did you know what it was?

Dana: I just knew that I had a purpose, and that was enough for me.

Dr. D: So you wanted to find out more about it?

Dana: It wasn't even that. My goal at that moment in time was to gain my independence. For that to happen, I had to convince the social worker who'd come to see me that first of all, I was never going to try to kill myself again. Second, I had to explain to her that I could no longer live with my mother. So my purpose at that point was liberating myself from a horrible situation. And although I was only

13, my near-death experience gave me the determination and strength to pull it off.

When I came back from that place of light, I had such conviction that I told the social worker that I'd never try to take my life again, because I'd seen the possibility of so much more to existence than misery, and that all my depression was gone. I've never been depressed since.

Dr. D: When you say, "I saw the possibility of so much more," what do you mean?

Dana: It was just that the veil was ripped away from my eyes, and I could see with perfect clarity that everything has its purpose, and it all flows together.

Dr. D: What happened next?

Dana: My social worker found a livable situation for me, and although it was still very difficult and I had a lot of trials to go through, I was at ease. Then she put me into modeling school, and I got a contract. I was discovered that same year, and the next thing I knew, I was traveling all over the world.

For the next 13 years, between the ages of 13 and 26, I became a mentor to those around me. It came very naturally because I was living my truth. I'd just come back with this clarity of living in my power, in authenticity, and everything was so absolutely clear to me. Things change, but one thing remains the same, and that's our truth—who we really are. The circumstances surrounding us may vary, but our ultimate reality never does.

Moreover, my NDE gave me the power to connect with others on a spiritual level, without all the ego getting in the way. I also lost all doubt and didn't really believe there was anything that I couldn't do. I think so many of us harbor fear, which can be paralyzing.

Dr. D: What do you think that fear is?

Dana: I think the biggest trouble we have is the fear of death. And it's a pity, because there's really nothing to be afraid of. Soon after birth, it seems to me, we start to lose our connection with our spirit. I think we come out full of life, and as we get older, we start to become conditioned and begin to lose that connection. As we diminish our spirit, the fear seeps in. It's attached to the ego and death.

Dr. D: So you think a lot of that has to do with the fear of death?

Dana: I believe that all of it does. I think everybody harbors a major fear of death.

Dr. D: And you lost that because you were so close to it?

Dana: I was there, and I saw that there was nothing to be afraid of—instead, I found only beauty. That's all there is in the world, and I understood that it's based on how we see everything around us. In that moment, the biggest thing that happened was being given the ability to change my perception of life. It's kind of like people who get to travel the world and see a bigger picture than those who stay home—it's an awakening.

Dr. D: You were very fortunate to have a near-death experience and see the light. Now, obviously, there's only a small minority of people who have that happen. What would you say to someone who hasn't gone through that? How can _they_ find their mission and purpose?

Dana: I think the answer lies within. If we can just be still for one moment and see the goodness that we all have inside ourselves, in our hearts—the Divine, or whatever you want to call it that's within—and simply allow ourselves to connect to our source, to our Higher Power, then all the fear washes away.

Dr. D: And then what happens?

Dana: And then as it goes away, the path opens up before us. You're one pebble on my journey, I'm one on yours, and that course is laid out before us. We're Divine— *we* are that Higher Power. When you realize that there isn't someone up there waiting to take this huge whip and knock you down, but that it's all love, then you can connect to that. You can do anything, and anything can come to you.

Dr. D: So when we can get out of the way, we manifest our destiny?

Dana: Yes, and as you remove yourself as an obstacle, people appear who are mirrors for you, because we show each other who we really are. These helpers will come to you all the time, and you'll be looking into the eyes of knowledge . . . into the eyes of love. Whatever you're working on, you'll gaze into that part of yourself when you look at somebody else. So don't be afraid to grow through those you meet.

That's the main thing I've learned with all my healing work: You have to be grounded to the earth and reaching for the stars at the same time. If you're living your passion, then all the power of the universe will spring to life to aid you in your purpose.

You Can See the Light

What's very clear to me after studying the experiences of people who have had NDEs, and which was made very clear to me in my own dream, is this: You don't need to have a near-death experience to see the light, but we all need some guidance, some rules to live by in order to fulfill our highest purpose in life.

You can discover your true identity and purpose in life—and find Heaven on Earth—by learning to live in harmony with what I call the New Golden Rules. By allowing them to unfold in your life, I predict that you'll find a deeper happiness than you've ever known or imagined, and you'll discover how to live in tune with your highest spiritual nature . . . and embracing this peace will help bring greater harmony to the world.

The four rules I'll share with you are progressive, meaning that each principle builds upon the previous one. It's a true evolutionary process where each rule (which includes points of action) depends in part on your implementing the one that came before it. The process flows, and you'll naturally spring from one step to the next until you effortlessly reach the final stage. But you don't have to wait until the end to experience bliss; you'll begin to know it in your life right from the start.

Let's embark on our journey in the next chapter by discussing the *old* Golden Rule.

CHAPTER THREE

Do Unto Others

As children, we all learned the Golden Rule at home, school, church, synagogue, or the like. I'm certain that you remember it: "Do unto others as you would have them do unto you." The basic idea is to do no harm; ideally, the original Golden Rule also encourages respectful and trusting relationships.

Every faith and tradition has its own expression of this principle:

- The poet Kabir wrote: "As you deem yourself, so deem others. Then you will become a partner to Heaven."

- In the Talmud, it is written: "What is hurtful to yourself do not do to your fellow man. That is the whole of the Torah and the remainder is but commentary."

- The Buddha also had a version of the rule: "Hurt not others with that which pains yourself."

- A great sage of India, Guru Arjan, wrote in the holy book of the Sikhs called the *Siri Guru Granth Sahib:* "Don't create hatred with anyone, as God is within everyone."

- And the Bible instructs: "Always treat others as you would like them to treat you; that is the Law of the Prophets." (Matthew 7:12)

There's no room for rudeness, selfishness, hate, or violence if we're treating our neighbors the way we want to be treated . . . or is there?

Do you think that there might be a connection between the fact that so few people experience bliss in their daily lives coupled with the concept that we find so few—even those who profess to be religious—who act as though they really love their neighbors?

Perhaps people don't treat others very nicely on a consistent basis because they don't treat *themselves* very well either. Many individuals, in my experience, act as if they don't love themselves very much at all. They don't take care of themselves or make the time to take pleasure in life or enjoy recreation. Perhaps they ignore their family members and spend way too much time hiding from themselves in work, or in other diversions such as sex, food, or drugs.

It could be that this is because they weren't cared for very well, especially when they were young. I've seen many patients, for example, who have the belief that they weren't nurtured as children; because of that feeling (correct or otherwise), they live with pain, anger, and resentment. According to the ancient laws of Eastern healing philosophy (which we'll explore later), this perception of not being taken care of as a child can create tremendous emotional imbalance. Medical research now shows that this can often lead to physical and mental illness. When people live in so much pain and carry with them such a tremendous amount of unbalanced stress, it's often difficult to relate to others with love, grace, and consideration.

I've meditated very deeply for a number of years about this difficult situation. This problem of lack of self-love and clarity isn't something I can dismiss easily, because it's continually being brought to my attention in my clinical work. Over and over again—regardless of the physical or medical reasons people come to me for a consultation—I continue to discover an underlying longing for spiritual evolution and the recognition, often on a subconscious level, that spiritual growth and greater self-love are the only ways out of misery.

During meditation I've asked my Higher Power: *How can people find happiness and bliss? How can I help them discover the Heaven on Earth that I found by living life with a spiritual foundation?* After all, having come from a divorced family and having gone through a difficult first marriage, I've also had pain and difficulty in some aspects of my life.

The answer God gave me was: "Meditate on Me and help others do the same."

So it's clear that we must all go through the process of spiritual development. During this journey, we encounter and transform the pain of the past, until finally we emerge from the tunnel of darkness to discover the bright light of God's love for us, and acknowledge all the blessings that we have deep within our souls.

During my close to three decades of medical and ministerial practice, I've witnessed countless people repeating the same negative behavior patterns over and over again. As I discovered that so many of us are searching for more spirituality in our lives, I was led to create this new set of Golden Rules. These are for those individuals who can perhaps use some direction in taking the next step in their own personal and spiritual evolution as human beings on this little planet we call Earth.

The New Golden Rules

Here is some basic information about the New Golden Rules. I'll discuss each of them in detail in the upcoming chapters.

New Golden Rule #1: Discover Your Miracle

Explore the path of right action in order to find your true identity—your Divine self. Realizing the miracle of your divinity requires three steps that will help you move from individual to group to universal consciousness. This process helps you unify your body, mind, and spirit with the infinite source of all creation. You'll realize your connection to the universe and the part you're meant to play in the unfolding of the spiritual evolution that is occurring in our lifetime. It's during this journey that you'll discover your miracle and plant the first seeds of living a more wonderful and blissful life.

The actions are:

1. Develop or deepen a regular spiritual practice.
2. Make selfless service an important part of your life.
3. Create a community of spiritually like-minded people.

When you take these three steps, you'll kindle the Divine spark that resides within your being and begin a unique process that will bring you great joy.

New Golden Rule #2: Listen and Agree

Once you've refined your life by initiating the actions above, you'll grow spiritually. After some time, you'll be able to recognize the pulse of the still, small voice within your soul and reap the magnificent rewards of allowing the mystical you to become the guiding force in your life. This voice within is the will of God for you, and it's there for you to know.

As you learn to listen deeply, the pulse of God's will for you will arise automatically and effortlessly. You'll be guided to your highest destiny by this manifestation from your awakened soul.

But it isn't enough to just hear the voice or feel the pulse of God's will for you. To fully reap the benefits of the second New Golden Rule, it's very important to agree to follow this voice's lead when you hear or feel it—that's the key to this principle.

New Golden Rule #3: Dissolve Your Blocks

After working with the first two rules, you're ready to evolve into your next level of spiritual development. This is an exhilarating process that I consider with humility, awe, and reverence. Each of you who is on the path to Heaven on Earth is beset by emotional obstacles, which are often unconscious, and keep you from advancing on your road to bliss. Everyone has these difficulties (anger, grief, and fear, for example), and they may also be the source of a great deal of pain and frustration in your life—for instance, you may feel as if you're stuck in a rut.

It isn't enough to simply recognize and try to transcend, or rise above, these blocks; it's better to dissolve them so that you can experience bliss on a daily basis. Among the keys to doing this are forgiveness, patience, and acceptance. After you receive the gift of these attributes, you'll find that the next step on the path awards you the even higher ideals of love, compassion, and royal courage. The development of these characteristics is the mark of enlightenment.

New Golden Rule #4:
See the Other Person As Yourself

This is the epitome of the New Golden Rules, for when you begin to see other people as yourself, you're able to see through the misperception of separation that we usually carry around with us. We often see others as apart from ourselves, but that's wrong: We're all one.

We also have the habit of feeling as though we're separate from God, but that's also a misunderstanding that began at birth. On a very subtle level, when we went through our mother's birth canal and entered the harsh reality of life here on this planet, we felt torn away from the One who sent us to fulfill our destiny. Although we may have lost the recognition of that reality, we all carry a spark of the Divine within us. Following the New Golden Rules helps you rekindle that tiny ember and turn it into the bright and beautiful flame of infinite love.

When you live this fourth rule, you once again transcend the feelings of pain, fear, and separateness brought about by simply being born. Once you see others as yourself—as a soul, just like you—your relationships will become more intimate, united, and harmonious.

Beginning to see the other individual as a soul lets you then see the Divine in all. And when you're able to recognize the Heavenly in yourself and in others, you also begin to notice a Higher Force in all things—from a beautiful tree to personal events that appear to be beyond your control.

It may take a day or it may take ten years, but one moment, with the grace of God, you'll have the realization that you're there. You'll remember who you are at the deepest level of your existence, experience the Divine love that resides within your being, and become yourself again.

Benefits of the Four New Golden Rules

These principles are simple to follow, although they do require a bit of discipline and practice. To receive the dividend, you must make the investment (so to speak), but once you decide that you wish to live a life of exaltation, you can easily do it—if you're committed to the process.

You've been drawn to this book because it's your time to move beyond the elementary school of spiritual development. *The New Golden Rules* will lead you to see the One in all, and help you appreciate the vastness of the cosmos.

As I'm sure you'll agree, these simple steps are deeply spiritual, yet don't require you to change your religion or the way you live your life in a dramatic fashion. For example, I'm not going to recommend that you drop out of society to go live in a cave somewhere, no matter how appealing that may sound at times! *You can discover bliss by simply learning to be yourself.*

The four new rules will lead you to a greater awareness of the truly finer, subtler things in your life. You'll feel grateful for every breath you take, realizing that this is the greatest gift of the Creator. When you develop this attitude of gratitude, you'll no longer take things for granted and will find new meaning, energy, and love in even the simplest acts.

Finding Purpose

The discovery of meaning in your life is perhaps one of the most significant benefits of following the New Golden Rules. Sociological research shows that those who are critically ill ask themselves two significant questions: *Did I have meaning in my life?* and *Did I love enough?* Many people, unfortunately, pass away without ever discovering or experiencing purpose in their life, which is a great tragedy and a source of major suffering during their last days on Earth. If you do achieve this, however, you'll "go home" in peace when it's your time to depart.

A physician colleague of mine was informed by his

dermatologist that he had malignant melanoma, an often-fatal form of skin cancer. He was jolted to his core and felt as if he were drifting above his body. Everything seemed unreal. Although he was in a state of shock from just being told that he had a serious illness, he went ahead and kept a date that night to attend a concert with his wife.

The evening was wonderful. He told me that it seemed as if he were floating on a cloud and that music had never sounded so sublime—as though he could not only hear the notes, but actually see them fly off the instruments in the orchestra.

Although such a heightened state of conscious awareness isn't sustainable, he's maintained a newfound gratitude for even the ordinary occurrences of everyday life. As we were talking, I almost felt as if I were in the presence of Buddha. My friend seemed to have a halo around his head—an aura that expanded as he told me his story.

Fortunately, his cancer was contained by a surgical procedure and never returned. But the night of his diagnosis, he learned a valuable lesson that's still with him today: Life is so precious that even the smallest, seemingly simple things deserve our awe. He now tries to take nothing for granted—his grandchildren's smiles and the dawn of each new day are causes for celebration. He's truly in bliss and has discovered a life of Heaven on Earth.

This man now shares his story with others in the hopes that they won't have to go through such a traumatic or fearful experience to finally slow down the rhythm of life and see it for what it is: a miracle in action.

As you progress on your path, you'll realize deep inside that the same force that causes the birds to fly south in the winter and return north in the summer guides your life as well. Your awareness of a power greater than yourself may have always been there, perhaps just out of reach, and now it will emerge often and unbidden.

When you incorporate these four simple New Golden Rules into your daily activities, life is smooth. You achieve greater success in your endeavors, and it comes to you easily and without resistance or struggle. You go to sleep at night with a special knowledge that all is well in your world, and you're deeply relaxed.

The Master Speaks

Once, a great master asked one of his brightest students, "My dear, sweet daughter, what is the secret of life?"

"To know God's will for you, sir, and to live to that will," she responded rapidly.

The old yogi, now reaching the end of his glorious life, stroked his long white beard and smiled brilliantly, his bright eyes glowing with love, light, and joy. As his student finished her sentence, he answered his own question: "To realize that God is everything, and to live in that flow."

We're all part of a vast river of life. When we live in unity and harmony with this flowing stream of energy, existence is bliss. We're as healthy, happy, and complete as any human being could ever hope to be. We're content, which leads to inner peace; and it's this quality that brings us to true and lasting happiness.

When we leave the flow and are out of touch with the depth of our own Divine spiritual nature, anguish and torment are invited into our lives. Quite often they bring their friends—fury, bitterness, and angst—which are all aspects of materialism and ego.

I want so much for you to be healthy, happy, and holy; to be able to reach out to others and share your gifts with them. It's my prayer that you'll feel the love of the universe flowing deep within your soul, and experience that joy and clarity every day for the rest of your long life.

In the Bliss

It's evening in the desert, as I sit outside in deep meditation. The passing dark clouds barely shroud a bright, full moon. As I gaze upward into the vastness, I merge with the glow of that Heavenly body as it comes out from behind a cloud. As I blend with the light, it seems to carry me away . . . away . . . away. . . . Breathing deeper and deeper, I go further into reverie.

I enter a timeless state where there's no past, no present, and no future. All my limitations are stripped away until only the truth remains. There's just one immortal essence of reality: the Creator who is the doer of all things. He is without anger, without fear; courageous, loving, and limitless.

Surfacing from this profound meditation immersed in the bliss of Divine well-being, I feel entirely complete within myself. I'm free, and I'm myself. I lack nothing in this bliss.

You can be complete, too, and feel the love. It's there for you now—all you have to do is reach out and take it.

As this chapter on our journey to the depths of an awakening soul closes, I want to share the lyrics to a song written by my musical partner, Master L, and the wonderful musician Wah! The song is called "Sahej," which means *effortless*. It depicts the thoughts, feelings, and experiences of someone who has discovered the power of his own Divine reality, the sweet caress of spiritual bliss.

Sahej

Oh Lord, I have come from wandering
If only for a moment I could know you
All my cleverness would vanish
So much is the power of the truth

Sahej, the easy acceptance
Sahej, of your own radiance
Sahej, the love of the Infinite
Enshrined in your heart and soul

The way is effortless

Now that I have found you
I'll keep you for all time
Hearing your name on the breath.
I feel your light
In every cell of mine

Sahej, the easy acceptance
Sahej, of your own radiance
Sahej, the love of the Infinite
Enshrined in your heart and soul

The way is effortless
The way is effortless

᷒

Recently, a man called to tell me that after many false starts he'd discovered his spiritual self. He sounded so much happier than I'd ever heard him. What was responsible for his newfound bliss? He'd started following the first New Golden Rule, which we'll discuss in more detail in the next chapter.

CHAPTER FOUR

The First New Golden Rule:
Discover Your Miracle

The first simple step to living a life of spiritual bliss is discovering the Divine miracle within us, for we're all unique. We all have our own special gifts and our own important mission that was given to our soul by our Creator when we agreed to take this human birth. The first New Golden Rule to living a life of Heaven on Earth—a life of satisfaction, contentment, and inner peace—is discovering that uniqueness.

More than 600 years ago a great master named Guru Nanak walked the old lands from Persia to India. He sang his lessons to local people as they gathered under a tree or by a riverbank to learn from this enlightened being. At the crux of his teachings was the idea that there's only one true immortal essence of reality, and that it's the same for everyone, regardless of whether they call themselves Hindu, Buddhist, Christian, Muslim, or Jewish. Guru Nanak called this true spiritual identity "Sat Nam," and he professed that it was within every one of us.

"Sat" means *truth,* and "Nam" means *essence* or *identity.* In his writings, Guru Nanak also called the Universal Spirit or God "Sat Nam." So, according to him and many subsequent spiritual teachers, it's the greatest truth that God is living within you. Many Divinely inspired masters have shared this same message: God and you—you and God—are one. That's the greatest miracle anyone could ever hope to realize.

The problem is that in the West, we've never before been taught to focus on this notion. In fact, the opposite is true: We've been programmed by our schools and religious institutions to believe that happiness, health, healing—and yes, even God—are all out *there* somewhere. We've been taught to look away from ourselves for all types of satisfaction. Many people seem to believe that their salvation lies external to themselves, but the greatest miracle you'll ever discover is that the reverse is true: God is dwelling within you.

A long time ago in a faraway place, a great king had a child. This baby was his firstborn son. When the boy was 18 years old, the king became ill and prepared himself to leave this earth for his Heavenly abode. He called his son to his bedside and told him, "My dear boy, I'm preparing to leave the earth. I want you to have the greatest gift in my kingdom, so I'm leaving you a small plot of land, which contains my favorite tree. There you'll sit and realize your destiny."

Being a dutiful son, the young man simply replied, "Yes, Father, as you wish."

After the king's death, the boy decided that he wanted to find his fame and fortune. He looked at the small piece of land with the one tree that his father had left him—and he wasn't impressed. After all, it was very small and surrounded by rocks. On several occasions, the boy even wondered why he'd been given this apparently worthless plot.

So one day, he set off to discover the world and seek his fortune elsewhere. He traveled far and wide searching and searching. Sometimes he wasn't even sure what he was looking for; he just hoped that he'd know it when he found it.

But alas, after two years of searching the world for his truth, he arrived home empty-handed. He was in a terrible mood and utterly dejected. Although he'd traveled near and far and looked high and low, he had nothing to show for it. He hadn't discovered anything—least of all his fortune, destiny, or truth.

Oh well, the boy thought, *at least let me pay homage to my father, the king, and go sit under his favorite tree.* So he did. As he was sitting and reflecting on his travels and current misery, he put his hand on the ground to pick up some dirt and run it through his fingers. Suddenly, his fingertips touched something hard, and then they ran across a number of similar firm objects. He lifted up a handful and looked at them. They were yellow and glowing.

The boy couldn't believe his eyes. He took a few and ran as fast as he could to the royal jeweler, and asked, "What do I have here?"

The royal jeweler took one look at the shining objects and told the young man, "You have a kingdom of riches, for these are the most precious gold pieces in your father's collection. No one knew where they were."

So the boy, who'd spent two years traveling hither and yon seeking his fortune, finally found it in the small plot of land his father had given him. He learned firsthand that the answers we search for aren't "out there" somewhere, but rather, they exist right where we are—we only have to look for them.

Your Path to Discovery

How can you discover your own miracle? How can you find your living divinity in the here-and-now? What can you do starting right away to begin the process of finding the precious fortune contained in your own Divine being?

Many people believe that their miracle can be discovered by thinking or intellectualizing, but according to Guru Nanak, thinking doesn't bring you even one step closer to self-realization: "By philosophizing, even a million times, the conception of God cannot be had."

Additionally, although a quiet mind is more favorable than one that's constantly chattering, neither silence nor stillness by themselves brings you closer to finding the God within. Obtaining immense wealth isn't the way to attain the truth or ultimate reality either.

So how can you begin the process of finding your true self, your own Divine nature that resides within your deepest being?

THE FIRST NEW GOLDEN RULE, PART I:
ENERGIZE YOUR SPIRIT

The first action to take to help you discover your miracle is to develop and sustain a regular spiritual practice. Swamis, sages, saints, and yogis call this regular spiritual practice "sadhana" (pronounced *sod na*), and without it, the chance of making progress on the spiritual path is dramatically reduced, if not impossible.

Yogi Bhajan once said, "Sadhana is the time you energize your soul," and I know from years of personal experience that he's correct—the experience is the highlight of my day. I've done a good sadhana since 1981, and I can tell you that I'd be a very different person without it—and that I never would have been able to accomplish my work over the years. Not only has it benefited me spiritually, but it has also given me a good dose of daily energy that helps me live at a very high level. A daily spiritual practice is at once reenergizing, rejuvenating, and resurrecting . . . it brings new life.

There are many examples of this process: Jewish people have their morning prayers, as do Muslims, Hindus, Buddhists, and Christians. Some people even use exercise (such as a morning jog) as a spiritual practice. It's all good, especially if the practice includes meditation.

A Natural Process for Health and Wholeness

Sadhana is a powerful and special way to lovingly nurture the Higher Power that lies deep within us. Our soul needs to be awakened to become the bright shining light of its full potential, just as coal needs to be put under tremendous pressure to become a diamond. Having a spiritual practice touches that deep stillness within your heart and pushes you along the path. It enlivens your timeless, eternal being.

Just as a farmer must prepare the ground for a harvest by removing the weeds, plowing the fields, irrigating the land, and especially sowing the seeds, so too do you, as a seeker of spiritual bliss, need to cultivate your mind to open your higher levels of awareness. Farmers don't expect to see the fruits of their labors appear in one day; they must do the work on a steady basis. Similarly, women or men who seek the Heaven on Earth of spiritual bliss can't expect to purify their minds in one day and enlighten their souls the next. Spiritual work needs to be done consistently.

As the farmer's plants must receive patient care after the seeds have been planted, and then again during the changes of season, so too must the person who wants to be in joy regularly cultivate the soil of enlightenment, patiently and with perseverance, by clearing his or her mind on a daily basis.

Here's another way to think about it: Just as you take a shower to clean your body, you must meditate to cleanse your mind of the residues of stress and negativity that pollute your thinking each day. Imagine not brushing your teeth or bathing for a few days. I doubt that you'd feel very good or be very attractive to others. Probably no one would want to be near you. It's the same idea with your mind, which must also be cleaned regularly. This allows you to be clear, sharp, and bright, and helps you function at a much higher level. It can make your mind strong, focused, and as brilliant as it can be.

A good sadhana spreads to all parts of your life. Slowly, you discover that you're making better choices about relationships, work, family, children, diet, and so on. Your attention to the spirit leads effortlessly to a life of greater pleasure, awareness, and success.

Hundreds of years ago, Guru Arjan wrote a poem that I love, and which I believe shares the same concept I'm describing: not looking outside yourself to discover your miracle, but rather going deep within. Here are his words:

> *All things are within the heart,*
> *The home of the self.*
> *Outside there is nothing.*
> *Those who look outside themselves,*
> *Are left wandering in doubt.*

Shake Hands with God

The tragedy of Western living is that we've never been taught how to look within ourselves for spiritual bliss. Even today, although many people know of these concepts, very few actually have been taught how to wake up in the morning and "shake hands with God." In my experience, only a small number of spiritual seekers have learned how to start their day in a positive way by doing a strong and consistent sadhana.

In fact, we're indirectly being taught the opposite. We've been programmed by television commercials to expect that the best part of waking up is having coffee in your cup—we're actually encouraged to believe that the most wonderful part of a new morning is stimulating ourselves with a caffeine rush so that we can tumble headlong into another day.

Does this resemble your typical wake-up routine? The alarm goes off and you stumble to the bathroom. After grooming, you have coffee and turn on the TV to hear all the bad news; or you read the newspaper, which also usually has a load of heavy negativity. Then it's off to work: You jump in your car and blast off down the freeway, fighting the morning traffic all the way to your job. Or perhaps you take a busy train or bus to work.

This daily routine is very stressful, and if left unaffected by a morning of meditation practice, it can have a negative impact on your entire day—not to mention your overall health. You end up going 'round and 'round like this for many years, until you die. Where's the bliss in that?

There's a better way: To realize the miracle of the one true essence of reality that resides within you requires a positive start each morning. The best part of waking up is *not* coffee in your cup—it's meditation in your mind. There's no better way to begin another glorious day of life than by raising your face to Heaven and shaking hands with God.

On many occasions over the past three decades, Yogi Bhajan discussed the great importance of regular spiritual practice, especially through morning yoga, meditation, and prayer. On June 26, 1990, he put it in the following way:

> You love your children? You do. They are beautiful
> . . . . Have you kissed the Soul? Have you hugged the
> Soul? Have you communicated with the Soul in the
> morning at the ambrosial hour when there is absolutely
> no disturbance? Sadhana is nothing but where a disci-
> plined one, the love, talks to one's Soul. Sadhana is
> nothing but where one prepares for the day to become
> kind and compassionate for everyone, including the
> enemies.
> When you stand, take a stand, and stand tall. Walk
> tall and stand by the strength of your Soul.

Shaking hands with God has a powerful impact. In fact, the amount of happiness in many people's lives is propor- tionate to their sadhana. Once, a little research project was carried out by Yogi Bhajan: When someone called with problems of any type—emotional, physical, or mental— they were asked if they were meditating on a regular basis. You can probably guess the answer. The people who were meditating regularly had fewer severe problems. Granted, although this isn't what you'd call a statistically significant scientific study, it's useful nonetheless in glimpsing the practicality of a daily sadhana.

Living Long and Well

Meditation brings you to a state of being where you are healthy, happy, and holy. Having a regular spiritual practice balances all areas of your personality and ensures that you feel great.

From a medical standpoint, it's known that those who meditate on a regular basis are healthier and live longer, too. This is very easy to understand. According to many recent studies involving the use of sophisticated x-rays (such as MRI and SPECT scans), meditation touches a place in the brain called the "happy spot." This point is connected to the immune system, which ensures better health. Meditation also touches the so-called God spot in your brain, which brings you the feeling of having your Higher Power close at hand.

This benefit extends the entire length of your life. The beauty of old age is being able to share your experience and wisdom with your family and community in order to make the world a better place for those who come after you. As you open up your heart and mind by practicing sadhana, your view of the material world will be replaced by one of higher spiritual values. Living these beliefs (which I'll discuss in detail later on) will allow you a better chance of creating a time of true peace on Earth and goodwill toward everyone.

If we look at the word *sadhana* and divide it up into its two parts, "sa" and "dhana," its meaning and power become quite apparent. "Sa" means *all,* and "dhana" means *blessings.* Therefore, when you do your sadhana, you receive all the blessings life has to offer.

When you make regular spiritual practice an action step to discovering your miracle, you systematically open up all your energy centers, or *chakras,* from the bottom to the top. In this way, you progress from self-absorption to living connected to all human beings. You develop universal or cosmic consciousness. Cosmic consciousness—feeling the oneness of everything in the universe—is a beautiful way to experience all of life's wonders. Here are the milestones you'll attain as you approach this heightened state:

— The **elimination of negative thinking** is the first benefit you gain from developing your sadhana. While the negative part of your mind is important from time to time when it helps keep you from taking an action that could lead you away from your highest consciousness, most people spend too much time dwelling on the negative. This imbalance robs you of pleasure and optimism. Sadhana restores mental balance and helps you keep things in perspective.

— With sadhana you also release your fondness of only thinking about success from an earthly or financial point of view. You start to realize that success can be spiritual as well, and you get the hint that you have a higher calling. Once that begins, you can see the pure potentiality of the cosmos in your daily life and begin the **development of a more creative, imaginative, and inspired way of thinking**.

— As you're able to see beyond the short term, you live from a higher energetic standpoint called "**empowerment.**" Here you're able to move beyond your need to control or manipulate situations or other people to a space where you can help them live their own greater good. Empowerment is a beautiful characteristic both from a personal perspective—you feel quite capable—and also from a collective-consciousness point of view. You can now begin to consider what you can do to help others rejoice in living a calm and balanced meditative lifestyle.

— As you gain time and experience in sadhana, your heart begins to open. There's an immense reservoir of love within you. It has just taken you some time to be ready to open up and experience all of it. Now that you've done this, you can discover the true meaning of love. You **become compassionate, kindhearted, and caring.** You can give of yourself to others with freedom from worry about what you may get in return.

— After you open you heart to the reality of love, you're ready to begin the adventure of higher living on your way to a life of Heaven on Earth. To live in bliss on a constant basis means that you must **discover and live your truth.** As you'll see in a later chapter, knowing and then living your truth is a fundamental requirement (and also a benefit) of spiritual living. Regular sadhana opens up your heart and then delivers to you the actuality of who you are. The secret is to then live it. You'll know you're living your truth when what you feel about yourself in the depths of your being is what you project to the outside world. If you aren't doing so, you aren't living well, because you essentially have a life of desperation and lies, which is an awfully painful way to exist.

To see if you're close to living your truth, you may find it useful to ask yourself the following three questions:

1. How do I see myself?
2. How do other people see me?
3. How do I want to be seen?

If the answers are reasonably compatible, you're in good shape as far as living your truth is concerned. Make sure that the way you think of yourself is the way others see you.

— After you discover your truth and begin to live it, you finally **find the beauty of true intuition.** This isn't knowing what someone's going to say or do, but instead is knowing the right action for *you* to take in order to fulfill your highest potential of living a Divine spiritual life. Regular sadhana brings you to this gift.

I know firsthand the power of true intuition. Once, I had to make a tough decision: I could stay home and play tennis every day, or I could go to Atlanta for an advanced-meditation workshop. I went ahead and decided to attend the course, and an interesting thing happened: During a break, I sauntered up to a table where some books were being sold. I was familiar with all of them except one. I opened the unfamiliar volume and immediately knew why I'd come to the seminar, because the book fell open to a page where I was able to find the solution to a question that I'd been contemplating for a long time. The answer seemed to fly off the paper and hit me right in the eye.

At that moment, I was grateful that I'd made the choice to favor my spirit. I had no expectation of what was to come when I decided to leave home. What happened can only be considered a true spiritual coincidence, what I call "synchro-destiny," which is an example of true inner knowing, or spiritual intuition, meeting practical behavior.

After you've released your negativity, become a creative person, learned to empower yourself and others, begun to live open-heartedly, and found a way to express your truth, you're pretty close to living in bliss. You're open, honest, and your highest self. You're dwelling in delight, feeling connected to all beings, and are ready to move beyond yourself to selflessly serve others. That's the power of sadhana—the first and most important action toward realizing your spiritual bliss.

The Master Speaks

A student asked the master a question about daily spiritual practice: "Sir, why do you do sadhana? After all, you're a master."

"Because I want to stay a master," was his reply.

Another student asked, "Sir, can I take a nap after sadhana?"

To this the yogi responded, "You can do anything you want after sadhana. I once ate a whole pizza after sadhana."

No one knows why the master says what he does. Perhaps he wanted to get the student's attention or make her laugh by saying that—or maybe he really did call for delivery! Regardless, the take-home message is clear: *"You can do anything you want after sadhana."*

Meditations on the Path

I invite you to experience a beautiful meditation. Why not do it as your sadhana every day for 40 days and see where it takes you?

Smiling Buddha Kriya

A *kriya* is an exercise complete in itself. This is a short and simple meditation to try first thing in the morning before your coffee.

- **Posture:** Sit in a comfortable cross-legged posture on the floor with your back straight. This is called "easy pose." (Alternatively, you can sit in a chair.)

- **Mudra (hand position):** With each hand, curl your ring and little fingers over and press them down with your thumb, keeping the first two fingers straight. Bring your arms up so that the elbows are pushed back and a 30-degree angle is made between the upper arm and forearm. The forearms must be parallel, with your palms facing forward. (You may have seen this hand gesture in paintings or statues. It is a position, or *mudra,* of happiness, and opens the heart center.)

- **Focus:** Concentrate on the point at the root of your nose between your eyebrows, which is called the "third-eye point." Breathe long and deep through the nose.

- **Mantra:** As you focus, silently chant the mantra, "Sa, Ta, Na, Ma." (It means "I am truth.")

- **Check in:** Make sure your elbows are pressed back and your chest is out.

- **Time:** Continue for 11 minutes.

- **To finish:** Inhale deeply through your nose, then exhale through your nose. Finally, open and close your hands several times and relax.

SMILING BUDDHA KRIYA

Historically, this is an outstanding kriya. According to the teachings of the golden chain of yogis that goes back thousands of years, this was practiced by both Buddha and Christ.

A great master who taught Buddha this meditation found him nearly starved and very unhappy. The Buddha was unable to walk after his 40-day fast under a fig tree. He began eating slowly as the great yogi fed and massaged him. When Buddha finally started smiling again, the master gave him this one kriya.

Jesus also learned this exercise in his travels, and it was the first of many that he practiced. If you love a man as great as he and want to earn his state of consciousness, it's important to follow what he did.

However, the purpose of your life isn't to *be* Jesus or Buddha—it's to learn to be *yourself.* Be a little selfish for your higher consciousness. Please master this technique and experience the state it brings, and then share it by creating beauty and peace. You can do this by reaching out to others, the basis of the second part of this New Golden Rule.

THE FIRST NEW GOLDEN RULE, PART II: SATISFY YOUR SOUL

The bliss state is one of a true and lasting happiness, which comes from contentment. A surefire way to find contentment is through service (or *seva,* as it's called in the original spiritual language) without thought of reward for yourself. The second action step for discovering your miracle, therefore, is to serve others. According to legions of spiritual teachers, this is one of the most important ways to attain higher consciousness, enlightenment, and bliss.

I remember one day when I was with Emma, the 72-year-old wife of one of my patients from Oklahoma. We were having a far-reaching discussion in my office in Tucson, and when we got around to talking about spirituality, she told me something that I'll never forget. It was so moving that I wrote it down and kept it until I could share it with you here:

"When I die and go to Heaven, God isn't going to ask me about my relatives, what kind of house I live in, or my bank account. He's going to ask me what I did for Him. How did I glorify His Name? That's the purpose of life."

Similarly, when asked by a student how to find God, the saint Neem Karoli Baba responded this way: "Serve people, feed people, and, for God's sake, stop thinking about yourself."

One of the greatest blessings of helping others is that it awakens the Divine energy within you. This has an interesting effect: You begin feeling the touch of your Higher Power guiding everything you do; thus, you realize that God is within you, and beyond that, working through you. You come to see that He is a working God who knows how to get the job done. So when you start to serve others without thought of reward for yourself, you turn on this sleeping giant within yourself. You then begin to effortlessly take the right action in your life, which leads you smoothly to Heaven on Earth . . . and bliss.

Perhaps one of the most interesting things about service is that it's an incredibly selfish act. In this case, though, I don't mean selfish in a bad way. It's just a simple law of nature: When we take one step toward the universe, it takes ten steps toward us. What you give must come back to you in the same way that what goes up must come down—it's a law of physics. In reality, nature abhors a vacuum. When you give, you create a vacuum, and Mother Nature must act to fill it, which benefits you.

My Revelation of Seva

I've had a number of personal experiences that help me understand this part of the first New Golden Rule. What I've learned is that the universe has a way of being very personal with you. God seems to know how to reach you in an individual way, so how I was rewarded for doing the right thing won't be the same way that you're rewarded for following your desire to serve somebody.

What I hope you'll see from my story is that who we're actually serving when we give is our own Highest Power. In my case, I certainly ended up doing so—and as you'll see, I was also helping humanity.

It happened after the Summer Solstice Yoga Camp I attended in New Mexico in 1995. After all the great activity of the week—yoga, meditation, camaraderie, delicious food, and so on—I was enjoying a fantastic natural high. On the last day of camp, Yogi Bhajan spoke to us about an upcoming trip to India that was to take place in September. I became so inspired that I told my wife, Kirti, "We're definitely going."

After coming down off the mountain where the camp was located, we stayed at the home of two very good friends. We were all discussing the upcoming India trip when I realized that Kirti and I just couldn't go. I'd recently left a very lucrative position as the director of the acupuncture, stress medicine, and chronic-pain facility at the University of Arizona's teaching hospital in Phoenix in order to move to Tucson and begin my new work helping people prevent and reverse memory loss. Our savings were starting to dwindle, and I didn't think we had enough money to make the trip.

One of our friends suggested, "Ask Yogi Bhajan."

"No, I don't think so," I replied.

We spoke about it for a few more hours and then decided to go out to dinner in Santa Fe. Guess who came in with around 20 people just when we were sitting down? If you said the yogi, you're right.

After dinner, we all got up to leave the restaurant when somehow I found myself walking next to the master with my friend on my other side. This is highly unusual because Yogi Bhajan usually has a huge entourage around him. But there we were.

"Ask him. Go ahead and ask him," my friend urged me.

After hesitating I began, "Sir, do you think . . . "

"You must go!" he finished my sentence.

I began again, "You think it would be a good—"

"It would be a *great* idea," he confirmed.

You'd think that would have been enough input to get me to sign up for the trip, but I still hesitated until a couple months later, when one of the yogi's personal assistants called and suggested, "You do so much for other people. Why don't you do something for yourself?"

Finally, just two weeks before the group trip was to embark, I sent in the money.

During this time, I'd also been working on the proposal for my first book, *Brain Longevity*. It seemed that I had just about everything tied up in that proposal: time, money, and possibly my professional future. A lot of energy and work had gone into preparing it, and things were down to the wire. My agent was actively pursuing the right publisher.

After my wife and I spent the night in a hotel room in Los Angeles readying ourselves for the morning flight to India, I received a call from my book agent in New York. He said casually, "I sold your book." Only he didn't just sell it— I learned that it had been bought by Warner Books for a very large advance. That was an awesome send-off to India for my wife and me!

But more great things lay ahead, as Kirti and I had an incredible trip. When we arrived in Amritsar, the holy city of immortality in northern India, and saw the Golden Temple (or *Harimandir,* home of God) for the first time, we both cried. This place is the holiest shrine of the Sikhs and a focal point for spiritual pilgrims from around the world. There, gazing up at that golden dome 15,000 miles from Tucson, we felt as if we'd finally come home. We kneeled down and touched our foreheads to the marble floor, and our eyes shone like stars in a pitch-black sky.

The Golden Temple is constructed half from marble and half from gold. It's a shimmering, glimmering sight that vibrates almost like a living entity. Over the past 400 years or so, sacred music has been sung there almost 24 hours a day.

On the morning of our third day there, I awoke with a deep spiritual insight—although similar to many profound occurrences in life, it now actually seems quite simple. This event is almost beyond explanation, but I'll try to put it into words. I had a personal realization of God's creative self, and clearly it was by His grace that I had this revelation. (I emphasize the word *realize* because it means more than to study, to intellectualize, or even to know.)

As I was strolling around the Golden Temple on the marble walkway, I had the perception that God was holding up a mirror for me to see myself. I actually saw my soul. Although it was more of a flash than a clear picture, I did have a good sense of my self. As I look back, I can say that it was like looking at a painting that was 50 percent finished, or perhaps tasting a meal that's only half done. It's not that I was upset by this—in fact, I was encouraged by what I saw. Nevertheless, I knew then that I had *a lot* of spiritual work to do in this life.

After many more enlightening experiences during that two-week journey to the center of our souls, we arrived back home in Tucson. As I was going through my mail, I saw an envelope from a lawyer I didn't know—that certainly seemed mysterious. It turned out the letter was from an estate attorney telling me that our nonprofit Alzheimer's Prevention Foundation had been left a huge sum of money by a woman who believed in our mission and had recently passed away.

As I step back and recall the unfolding of these events, I see the hand of God working. I took one small step toward my Higher Power in faith that everything would be all right, and God blessed me many times over. Never in my wildest dreams did I expect what happened in any aspect of our trip or upon our return home. I went to India in innocence, almost like a child—in a very real sense, I *was* one as I experienced something grand for the first time.

I think that God talks to us and guides us in some ways that we do understand, and sometimes in ways that we certainly don't—but all this guidance serves the higher good. I believe that God blessed me with money in this case because that's what I needed at that time, and especially because that's what I'd understand. If there would have been something else that would have had a greater impact on me at that point, then that's probably how God would have gotten my attention. In this case, however, money definitely worked.

But, beyond that, the funds God gave us because we served our Higher Power were used again to help others through our foundation. Since then, my wife and I have been grateful many times over for the gift of enlightenment we received during our trip to India, and thankful again to have the opportunity to share this blessing with others through seva.

Service and Your Health

From a medical-science point of view, selfless service is good for you. Recent research tells us that altruism lowers stress chemicals and improves many aspects of health, from immunity to brain function.

One patient of mine with severe chronic fatigue syndrome would agree. After searching around the country for a doctor who could help restore her to optimal health, she went home to San Francisco. There she undertook a volunteering project—and that's what brought her wellness. She now reads to disadvantaged children in her public library three times a week and credits that service with helping her heal.

According to the recent medical research I mentioned, she's correct: Helping others without attachment to any reward for yourself improves your mental, physical, and emotional health. It produces what scientists call "the helpers' high." This phenomenon is distinguished by an increased blood level of powerful disease-fighting immunological cells in your body, as well as an abundance of happiness-producing chemicals (such as serotonin) in your brain.

How to Get Started with Seva

Apparently, Americans like the idea of volunteerism. It was recently noted in a newsletter I received from an organization that does research on selfless service that 44 percent of Americans volunteer their time. That translates to more than 80 million people helping others.

Can you think of a way that you can apply this important

lesson to your own life? You may assume that what you do to serve others has to be something on a grand scale, but it doesn't—it can actually be quite simple. Your intention should be to fill a need, and your giving should also be an act of joy. The intention to make another happy should be there as well. As time passes, you'll see that all this will play out on a subconscious level as it becomes second nature for you to give of yourself to others.

In the beginning, however, you may have to concentrate on what you want to give as well as receive. If you yearn for love, give it to others; if you want joy, learn to bring it into someone else's life; if it's money you desire, give it away to a worthy cause or work with someone else to develop their affluence. I do this by helping beginning authors learn the tricks of getting published, such as writing a book proposal, finding an agent, and then a publisher.

The simple ways of serving are often the most profound. If you want good health, help others regain theirs. If you want to be blessed, learn to bless someone else. Don't worry—you can develop this capacity. I work on doing so often, as I offer a person I meet a silent prayer for well-being. You see, God shows no favorites; He listens to everyone.

Service Through Giving

Another (perhaps less obvious) way to bless and serve people is to honor them with a gift. My Italian wife is a sweet example of putting this into practice: Whenever we go to someone's home, she always offers a present, such as a pretty piece of pottery or a nice bowl of fruit. When I go to a foreign country to speak, she brings something for our sponsor. Everyone loves receiving a gift, especially when it's unexpected. If you can't think of what to give someone, try bringing that person a flower. If you've never done this before, you'll be pleased to notice how happy a simple treat—a fragrant rose, for example—can make someone feel.

As you give, so shall you receive . . . and that's the miracle of this process. As you gain this knowledge, you'll find that the more you contribute, the more you get in return—and then you'll want to give and give and give! This satisfies your soul because your true nature is that of God, and God is just like the sun: His light shines on everyone. So be like this yourself, and shine your spirit on one and all. As the Buddha said: "Hope for everyone to be happy, then you will be happy, too."

Judaism is also rich with the idea of giving to others. One concept in this tradition is called "Tikkun olam," which means repairing, mending, or improving the world. People of the Jewish faith are responsible for not only their own well-being, but also for the rest of society. In line with this, Jewish children are taught that they have a responsibility to help make the world a better place.

It just makes sense that if you see yourself in the image of God, you'll act responsibly to help the world, so the Torah teaches about *gemilut hasadim,* or acts of loving-kindness. This is akin to doing something for another without expectation for repayment, or receiving anything in return. You're asked to give a blessing to another with a joyous heart.

Giving at Work

As you enjoy the bliss of giving, you'll find that it seeps into places you may never have thought it would. One of them is your job. If your occupation is your passion, and your passion is your work, then you're truly blessed. For many people, however, this isn't the case. Their job is a pain; it's drudgery. The most effective way to remove the grind from your workplace—and thus, your life—is to channel the Infinite into your work.

The following story is a great example of how labor can become joy as you channel your soul's love, set free through the service of giving, into your activity.

A few years ago, three saintly men stayed at our home in Tucson. They were *ragis,* or singers of sacred music. The leader, a gentleman named Bhai Avtar Singh Ragi, was a man of about 75 years who'd done this work his whole life. Not only that, his entire lineage had the same vocation. For 13 generations—more than 500 years—they'd sung songs for seekers of truth all over the world.

Our guests awoke early every morning to chant a particular morning prayer. Unfortunately, Tucson has a relatively small spiritual community of this nature, so not that many folks came to hear them sing. Only about four or five people were there to enjoy the greatest sounds of this type of music in the world. On the third day, I approached their leader to apologize for the poor turnout. He then shared something that changed my life.

He told me that when his teacher (who also happened to be his granduncle) was preparing to leave his body, the elderly man called him to the bedside and said that whether there was one person in the audience or 1,000, he was singing for God.

When the ragi told me that, I immediately "got" it, and felt the glory of the concept settle down into the deepest part of my being. My feeling is that if we can develop ourselves to the point that we can learn to live in that vibration where we're channeling our Higher Power into everything we do—and if we can remember that we're "singing for God," no matter what form our gift of service takes—then there can be no drudgery in our work life. There can only be the blessings of the One immortal essence of reality working through us.

Practically Speaking

Part II of this first New Golden Rule will help you with seva, but please also remember to do your sadhana before you go to work. This will ensure that you're in a higher vibration when you're around your co-workers. After following your daily spiritual practice, notice how you're serving others on the job.

When you're actually present in the moment and are clear about your service to others, you feel much better about what you're doing. As your work becomes more of a gift, it becomes less of a chore and less draining. After a while, if your current profession isn't the correct thing for you to be doing—if it isn't the right action for you be taking to reach your highest destiny—you'll find that it will fall away or change effortlessly, and you'll be guided to the right work.

One of the most beautiful expressions of soul satisfaction through service was given by the Nobel Prize–winning Indian poet, Rabindranath Tagore, who wrote:

I awoke and saw that life was service.
I acted, and behold, life was joy.

Misery arises from indulging in selfishness. In contrast, the ultimate satisfaction and gratification of your soul comes from helping others. What you do out of Divine love remains inscribed in your heart forever. As spiritual people, we're all here to serve, uplift, be graceful, give hope . . . and give the very deep love of our soul to all those in need. The happiness that you seek will come from your best wishes for the welfare of others. When you serve others with no concern for results, you are a true person of spirit.

THE FIRST NEW GOLDEN RULE, PART III:
ENJOY THE COMPANY OF THE HOLY

In concert with the development of a consistent sadhana and the practice of seva is spending time with a community of like-minded people. Having a community—a congregation or a "sangat," as it's often called in Eastern spiritual circles—helps you further solidify your relationship with your Higher Power.

One of my favorite sayings is: "Kundalini surji sat sangat." This saying means that the *kundalini* energy rises in the company of the holy. Kundalini is that healing vibration produced by yoga, breath work, meditation, and prayer, which goes up your chakras to enliven your brain and mind. It also raises your consciousness and helps you reach your full potential as a human being.

Because it increases your kundalini, being around like-minded people who support your quest for spiritual development helps you increase your inner strength and raise your energy level. You simply feel fantastic around your group because your superficial behavior patterns drop away as your true being is expressed. Under usual sangat circumstances, you're fully accepted as you are, rather than being judged.

A sangat can be thought of as an extension of your family and a social-support system, which I believe is very important to have as you grow spiritually. We're all part of the family of humanity, and according to both Eastern healing philosophy and Western thought, group energy—be it from family members, friends, or church or synagogue members—is a very important part of well-being and living in the light.

Anyone who has ever meditated in a group setting, gone to a really great religious service, or enjoyed the power generated by a choir in a gospel church can attest that spiritual vibrations are multiplied when you surround yourself with those who support your energy rather than drain it. Connection, trust, and love are what we all need to be at our best. As we come together in community, the bonds that we create with our extended spiritual family create deeper meaning in our lives. In this way, having a sangat helps you go through life with peace and tranquility.

The group energy you receive by surrounding yourself with like-minded individuals is similar to the unconditional love that you receive from a happy, well-functioning family. Many people have told me that they always feel their best when they're around their sangat, especially because of the love and kindness they're able to give and receive in that cozy environment. I encourage you to wholeheartedly embrace the warmth and comfort of others on the path. This practice creates the family that we carry inside of us; it's a safe haven in our intense and often troubled world.

I remember very well experiencing the power of the sangat firsthand when I started on my spiritual journey of becoming an American Sikh and yogi back in 1981. I also learned that the nurturing energy of a group doesn't mean the exclusion of everyone outside that circle.

Two good friends whom I'd grown up with and roomed with in college had also moved to Albuquerque. But after I met my spiritual teacher and started practicing yoga on a regular basis, it became clear to me that I needed to be around my new group while I grew my beard, started wearing a turban, and developed a strong, consistent sadhana. So for two years I chose not to see my old pals very much, since they had a different lifestyle.

After I gained confidence in my new life path with the help of my sangat, I was able to rekindle those friendships. Today, I'm very happy to report that we remain close, talking on the telephone frequently and getting together whenever possible. (Coincidentally, both of my grown children are very good friends with the son of one of these men.)

Supported to Wellness

One example of the power of group energy that's had great success for more than six decades is Alcoholics Anonymous (AA). At AA meetings all over the world, people are able to connect with others who share the same desire to stop drinking. Those who attend also make a commitment to a spiritual life and helping others because they realize that this is their best chance for a healthy lifestyle. Moreover, they find through experience that meditation, prayer, group support, and service are very important keys to living a spiritual life.

By the same token, recent research from Stanford University School of Medicine discloses that women with breast cancer who participate in group therapy have a higher quality of life. There's also some intriguing evidence for the idea that this same communal support also leads to a better survival rate among cancer patients. Additionally, it's been shown that having a social support network of family members, friends, or sympathetic co-workers is strongly associated with overall heart health, a lower risk of recurrent heart attacks, and increased longevity. These studies all point to the inherent healing force of sangat.

The Power of Group Prayer

Quite often, when one member of a group falls ill, those in their sangat will pray for them, either individually or perhaps together. Research by medical scientists has shown how powerful this is. In one study, prayers from friends in a church congregation lowered the risk of dying from heart surgery by 700 percent. You read correctly: *700 percent!*

This tremendous healing power was brought home to me when I had a serious illness, and it was the prayers of my sangat that got me back on my feet. I was humbled by their love and distinctly felt the effect of their energy while it was directed toward me. I remember the exact moment when I received a very clear message that I was healed: I later discovered that this time coincided exactly with a group meditation and prayer organized by a friend of mine.

I've also witnessed the profound healing experiences of others at various meditation sessions I've led around the world. This doesn't just impact physical issues, but also psychological and relationship situations as well. I recall that after a beautiful meditation at a conference in South Carolina, a woman told me that she felt as though she'd healed a difficult relationship with her daughter. I found out later that this had actually occurred.

I'm blessed to participate in a delightful regular healing circle that takes place every Wednesday night at the Sunstone Healing Center in Tucson. Many people, such as those surviving cancer, tremendously enjoy these powerful sessions. At the end of this chapter, I'll share the dynamic healing meditation we do there. It combines the concept of service (you're giving to others as you send them positive healing energy) and the concept of sangat (it's usually done in a group, although it can also be effective when practiced alone).

I'm grateful to have the opportunity to be part of these sessions because there's a tremendous outpouring of positive healing intention, energy, and love directed to each member of the group, as well as to other people who are in need. We also collectively bless our planet with peace and harmony.

After exploring scientific literature on the subject and experiencing the power of group energy, I can say without reservation that there's no other factor in medicine that can ever have a greater effect on the quality of your life, your recovery from an illness, or your longevity than the love and prayers of your community.

Developing Sangat

Let's explore a few ways that you can develop or expand your own group of like-minded people. One simple method is to attend a yoga class. At a weekly or biweekly session in your community, you'll meet new people, and you and your yoga friends will have something spiritual in common. This is a great way to expand your circle. Remember that *yoga* means "union," so you're not only uniting your own mind, body, and spirit, you're also uniting your soul with those of your classmates. Often, these new acquaintances develop into deep and lasting friendships because they have a spiritual foundation.

Or perhaps you can create a sangat by offering yoga instruction yourself. What better way to develop a community than to teach? You can create a class that reflects your spirit by allowing participants to share their feelings before you begin, and by spending time together afterward simply chatting, drinking tea, and enjoying some fruit or cookies. This is a lovely way to become part of a new group of like-minded people.

If you're a spiritual seeker but yoga isn't your cup of tea, another great way to meet individuals who are also looking for growth is by attending a gathering at your house of worship. Perhaps there's a Bible class or another discussion group where you can make new friends.

For example, at a particular Jewish temple in Miami, people gather with a cantor who plays a guitar and sings lively spiritual songs in their tradition. I know of many individuals and couples who get great satisfaction out of attending such gatherings.

Your First Steps

The great Chinese philosopher Lao-tzu said that a journey of a thousand miles starts from beneath one's feet. Sometimes that voyage begins with a huge step, and sometimes it's a small one. The key to walking the path of an enhanced spiritual life is to begin right where you are by developing your sadhana, reaching out to others, and finding your group of like-minded people who are also on the journey to bliss. In this way, you can start to move from your individual self to group consciousness, which takes you to Infinity.

Connect with yourself first, and you'll do the same with those around you. When that happens—when you're in touch with the Divine within yourself and feel it in others—then you'll automatically be connected to the Divine within all beings. You'll discover your highest reality, and God will come to sit in your heart.

Meditations on the Path

This highly effective meditation deals with *vayu siddhi,* the power of air. This allows you to send your loving intention and powerful projection past the perception of separation we so often have. In reality, we're united, and this meditation enhances that quality. It also brings about great health and many other desirable positive changes.

Meditation to Heal Self and Others

Strive to maintain your chant at full volume (loud, but not raucous) throughout the meditation.

- **Posture:** Sit in a comfortable meditative posture, in "easy pose" (see page 47), on the floor or in a chair with your back straight.

- **Mudra:** Place your hands parallel with and facing the ceiling; fingers are together and pulled down. Your elbows are snug at your sides with the forearms in close to your upper arms. Position your hands at a 60-degree angle, halfway between pointing forward and to the sides.

- **Focus:** Close your eyes ninth-tenths of the way.

- **Breath:** Inhale completely through your nose before you start chanting, and don't exhale for one complete cycle of the mantra. If you run out of air, simply sniff in a little more through your nose.

- **Mantra:** "Ra Ma Da Sa, Sa Say So Hung." (It literally means, "The service of God is within me.") This should be sung in one complete exhalation. As you chant the first "Sa," your navel point should be pulled in so that this syllable is abbreviated. Then rest for four beats between the first and second "Sa."

- **Time:** Perform this meditation for 11 minutes. Very gradually (over a period of years), the time may be increased to a maximum of 31 minutes.

- **To finish:** First inhale deeply through your nose. Hold your breath and send *yourself* positive healing energy. (You can direct it to a specific spot if you wish.) Be as focused as a laser beam . . . and then exhale.

  Next, inhale deeply, hold your breath, and visualize the person to whom you want to send healing. Make that image in your mind very clear, and see a glowing green light around the person. Exhale as you keep that vision strong; and then take another long inhalation, hold your breath, and continue to send the person green healing energy. Still keep the picture in mind as you exhale.

  For the last time, inhale deeply, hold your breath, and see the person very clearly. Witness the green healing light washing over them and bathing every cell in their body. Exhale and relax.

MEDITATION TO HEAL
SELF AND OTHERS

A short poem by the great master Guru Arjan beautifully sums up the tremendous power of sangat:

I have totally forgotten my jealousy of others
Since I found the company of the holy.
No one is my enemy, and no one is a stranger.
I get along with everyone.
Whatever God does, I accept as good.
This is the sublime wisdom I have obtained from the holy.
The One God is pervading all.
Gazing upon Him, beholding Him
I blossom forth in happiness.

Now that you've discovered your miracle, you're ready
to learn how to take the next step in living a life of bliss. To
do that, you'll explore the process of listening for the still
small voice of the Divine within your being. As you'll soon
see, however, it's not enough to listen for—or even hear—
this sound. There's something else you must do to live the
second New Golden Rule, and that's what I'll explain in the
next chapter.

CHAPTER FIVE

The Second New Golden Rule:
Listen and Agree

*H*ere I am, awake in the <u>amrit vela,</u> the "time of nectar" in the early hours of the morning, preparing for sadhana. Before I begin my morning meditations, I think of a line I read long ago that said that the soul finds freedom in action. I remember those words during this remarkably beautiful June morning in the desert as I see so many little animals scurrying about outside my window in search of a delicious breakfast. There are bunny rabbits, gophers, and even a few lizards.

Most of all I notice the colorful birds flying around, landing on low tree branches or ocotillo bushes. One in particular draws my attention: It appears to be a quail pecking at a desert flower and shaking fruit from the plant's rough, well-guarded leaves. Finally, she retrieves and eats the bright yellow morsel. Then the bird simply flies away, probably looking for another piece of food from an equally ready bush. It looks to me as if *these little creatures are all totally in touch with their souls. They're finding freedom in natural action.*

I note how balanced and perfect all this is—no wasted motion, no lost effort. The winter turns to spring even here in the desert, and spring turns to summer. The flowers bloom; the animals hunt; and the birds make their nests, raise their young, and eat the flowers. It's all so absolutely normal and natural. . . .

Our True Selves: Loss, and the Desire to Regain

Like the rest of the world, we human beings are also born in perfect balance. When we're infants, we're full of love, trust, and grace; we're shining and happy souls. Yet with life being what it is, we seem to lose our equilibrium and stability over time. As we grow up, we're taught many things designed to bring us into the fold, yet this modification (which, of course, has somehow evolved to keep order on the planet) takes us away from the purity of our innocence.

Over the years, it's likely that we may lose our center as we try to conform to the reality of our circumstances. It happens so imperceptibly that we don't even notice it until a life-transforming event—perhaps an accident, illness, or loss—brings our attention back to who we once were, and in reality, who we really are. I've come to know that it's when we lose our center and hit the sides of the bank on our flow through the river of life that we suffer from pain and negativity. Even more important, it's when we regain our true inner nature that we're free.

The secret of regaining our innocence, our center, and our spirit is to find the way back to living a natural life in balance, and to thereafter stay in that flow. But how can we do this? How can we ever free ourselves from the cycles of painful experience that may have become part of our lives? How can we take the next stride in our search to understand the real purpose of our existence?

You can certainly think about it, and many of us spend a lot of time thinking and intellectualizing about lots of things. But according to the writings of the ages, neither thinking nor philosophizing will ever bring you one step closer to discovering the truth about yourself and your relationship to your Higher Power. You may possess myriad intellectual subtleties, but not one of them is of any avail in attaining the Ultimate Reality that you seek.

And while some speak of stillness, silence of the mind is rarely attained long enough to tune in to the essence behind the mask that most individuals wear. Moreover, although it's certainly worthwhile to try to be in the moment (for that's really all we have), it's quite difficult to do so consistently because of all the static in our mind and environment. I know of many spiritual seekers who have been on the path for a long time, yet they still find it a great challenge to "be in the now."

How, then, can we become self-realized? How can we smash through the veil of falsehood?

Open Yourself Each Morning

The very first step is sadhana, which we've discussed in great detail. It's through the practice of regular yoga, meditation, and/or prayer in the early hours of the morning that we place ourselves in a more receptive position. It helps open the door to liberation from the mistaken idea that we control the flow of our existence, which is our ego talking. The truth is that we have no control, and all occurrences are by the grace of God. We can simply help move things along, and we begin with sadhana (which leads us to seva and sangat).

The purpose of daily spiritual practice is to clean the mind of refuse, as a dentist drills out a cavity. Your morning practice will clear your mind so that the voice of God can come through and guide you in your life. You can learn to listen for it and follow its direction wherever it leads you. You'll first follow the voice through faith, and then as you experience more inner peace, your devotion to listening to this internal guidance—and agreeing with it—will grow.

Yet it's in that initial faith that you'll hear His voice, which can move mountains. Without that faith and belief that God does want to talk to you and has a plan for your life, even pebbles may seem as heavy as boulders. In my experience, when you get to the place of being able to tune in to Divine guidance (which is God within yourself), everything you need flows to you, and you find a magnificent palace of peace and contentment within your heart.

Deep Listening and Acceptance

Hearing is something that happens automatically as long as your ears are healthy. To really *listen,* however, requires cultivating concentration and learning to pay attention. It involves being patient, and perhaps most important, suspending judgment about what you hear. As you become a good listener, you become aware of the message beyond the words and learn how to tune in to the heart of the individual speaking. You also pick up subtle cues and feel the vibration of the other person. Deep listening is really about tuning in—being aware of the acoustic energy in your environment.

These attributes are also critical when you listen for the voice of God and want to appreciate His will for you. We all have a basic need to understand and be understood, and God also wants this. The best way to comprehend—be it another person or your Higher Power—is to listen carefully, which requires discovering what lies inside our deepest self.

Sometimes you may hear the voice of God, but you don't want to accept it. That's why you must not only *listen,* but also *agree* to follow the instructions and not judge, over-analyze, or label. Those impulses are your ego talking again, and have nothing to do with God, Who is nothing but truth and justice given to you at the correct time and in a safe space. You may not care for what that voice tells you to do, but I've learned that it's best to simply obey.

Most of the time, however, you'll love and be amazed by what you hear, recognizing it as strong and true and reveling in the awe of His majesty. You'll probably say something like, "Yeah, that's right! *That's* what I need to do."

Tune In for Bliss

If you spend a lot of time and energy overanalyzing life, you're going to miss out on a lot, especially the way God is working with you. Sometimes it's difficult to actually hear a voice. I think it's important to listen attentively, but I know that it doesn't always appear—at least not on a regular basis. For example, as I mentioned, I've actually heard God's voice only a handful of times. Although those moments were exceedingly transformative, it's always good to have a back-up plan.

For many seekers, a good strategy is to become guided by the *pulse* of the voice—the will of God for you, which resides within your heart and soul. You can allow the Higher Power's vibration to manifest in you and shine through you, and then your actions can arise from that pulse.

What do I mean by that? Let your actions flow natural-ly from your meditative mind—in other words, do your sad-hana, serve others, surround yourself with like-minded peo-ple, and let it flow. As Jiminy Cricket said so wisely in *Pinocchio,* "Let your conscience be your guide." When you agree to follow God's intention for you by following your conscience, you'll discover that you know His will for you because you'll feel very calm, cool, and collected. Even if what you interpret as His message seems dramatic, such as moving to a different city, changing your job—or as in my case, changing publishers—you'll do it because you feel real-ly good about your decision. You'll be at peace with it, and *that's* how you'll recognize it as God's will.

You see, one of the most beautiful ways in which God speaks to us is through inner peace. This deep sense of inter-nal harmony confirms that the message is truly from Him. It was Jesus who said, "Peace I leave with you. . . . Do not let your hearts be troubled, neither let them be afraid." If you feel closer to bliss, you're following the right path. If you feel agitated by your choice, perhaps you need to reevaluate your decision.

You can also think of this in terms of a baseball analo-gy: If you feel peaceful about the message you hear or the decision that you're about to make, it's safe. If it doesn't feel right after you meditate on what you feel and consider is the correct action for you to take, then it's an out. Above all, remember that you're to be led by peace. It's as simple as that.

I learned this firsthand from my teacher. Once I had an offer to change jobs, and it felt like a really good opportunity, but it required quite an adjustment, including moving to a new city. I wanted Yogi Bhajan's opinion, so I sent him a letter outlining all the facts: how much more money I'd be making, what my new position and title would be, and a few more details about the proposed switch.

When I saw him, he asked me only one question: "Do you feel good about it?" I did, so I made the change. If I hadn't felt an inner peace about the move, I wouldn't have taken the new position. Interestingly, this change in my life—which seemed overwhelming at the time—has led to a tremendous amount of positive personal and professional transformation, including being able to write this book.

God is creativity in action, and sometimes I think it's all like a big chess game. He's thinking and acting maybe five or six moves ahead, at levels way beyond our perception. But when we look back at a sequence of events, it certainly makes sense, and beyond that we can see the fingerprints of God in action as He guides our life.

Recognizing Karma

When you become a good listener with respect to what God has to teach, you'll derive a great deal of spiritual benefit and will understand your *dharma*, or purpose, in life (which I'll talk about later in this chapter). This concept is the opposite of *karma*, which is what occurs when you repeat actions that keep you at a certain level of existence. Karma is cause and effect (although it's not necessarily good or bad—it can be either or both), but it can really slow or even stunt your spiritual growth because you may repeat the same mistakes over and over again. Living a life of repeated "lower actions" keeps you from realizing your higher spiritual self. The following story is an example of how this can happen:

Once I advised a 77-year-old man named Max who was wealthy, in fairly good health—and very unhappy. He came to see me because of low energy and mild depression, and after talking to him and checking his energetic pulses, it was easy for me to see the problem.

Max had a rough relationship with his mother. They argued a lot, and as a youngster, he'd get depressed after these fights. He'd had three marriages, as well as many business relationships that were all difficult because they followed the same pattern. In his relationships with his wives, for example, he'd first be in what he called "neutral." Then he'd start an argument, which would leave him feeling quite low. After a period of rest—sometimes literally requiring three days in bed—he'd again be in neutral and approach his wife for a brief period of harmony before the pattern began all over again. He did the same thing in his business life: He created conflict from peace.

His often-repeated actions (which were out of his awareness), caused the same negative effect to occur over and over again. As you can probably guess, he achieved very little personal or spiritual growth in his life. But he *did* have a glimmer of light shining within him, as we all do, and his soul's prayer was answered when God brought him to see me. (It was also a blessing for me, because I learned a lot from him, and more important, I was able to serve his spirit.)

Max was amazed when I pointed out how he created this same situation over and over again, because it was the same pattern he'd experienced with his mother. When I explained that he did this because it made him feel loved, he was further amazed—and also confused because he didn't understand how this could be. I then pointed out that as unpleasant as it was, his relationship with his mother meant love to him, because for all of us, our mother is our first source of affection—and a very powerful one at that. What he was doing was trying to feel the love of his mother.

After he thought about my conclusion for a moment, he looked at me and said, "Dr. Dharma, I've spent 20 years in therapy at a cost of $200,000, only to learn all I needed to know from you in 20 minutes." Thereafter, using a special meditation that I shared with him, counseling, and self-assessment, he was able to change his behavior and really enjoy life for the first time. He released the past and found his future.

Moving Toward Dharma . . . and Bliss

In everyday life, karma exists when you act in order to satisfy your ego (whether you realize it or not), and it involves paying off universal debt. When you live your dharma, however, you rise above the notion of karma, because you no longer create that burden. You're vibrating in accordance with higher values, which leads to profound spiritual growth.

Dharma is what you do for others; it's your Higher Self

in action. The second New Golden Rule can help with this, because when you're able to hear God's voice, you're drawn to live your dharma. Your Higher Power doesn't want cause and effect, only bliss. When you listen for and agree with God's will for you, you transcend karma and become independent of it. Dharma, therefore, *eliminates* karma—that is, your regular meditation practice and desire to hear God's voice washes away the stains of this cycle from your soul.

Dharma devours this burden because your choices become much more refined. You're more conscious of your Higher Self in your daily life and choose actions that are positive for you and your family, as well as the universal community. That's what is meant by the Buddhist concept of "right action," and it brings about bliss.

To live an exalted spiritual life of dharma and bliss requires you to surrender to the guiding pulse in your soul. You become still as you listen and feel the love well up from deep inside your heart. As you elevate yourself by listening, you become blessed with many praiseworthy qualities, such as thoughtfulness, understanding, compassion, acceptance, and tolerance. You develop a sixth sense, because as you favor the pulse, you're drawn—sometimes unconsciously— toward the correct action. The franticness or frenetic feelings in your mind that you may have endured in the past are released, and with the dismissal of this furious distraction, suffering and pain retreat.

Even someone who's never thought of becoming spiritual or has no experience with it can find his or her true path by following the pulse of God's will. If you learn to listen and agree, and then to act on that vibration, the meaning for your life will soon become apparent, and you'll be shown the way—despite sometimes feeling hopeless and blind when it comes to the direction of your destiny. And even if you think that you haven't found the way to achieve fulfillment, you'll discover the path to liberation from your negativity and live in bliss as you discover the right action for you—all based on listening for His voice. As you learn to hear within and become devoted to the experience, you'll see that your repeated mistakes become fewer as your actions become one with His will.

The Healing Power of Faith

Listening for and then hearing the will of God in your consciousness is one thing. The other aspect of the second New Golden Rule, which is really of equal (if not greater) importance, is *agreeing* with the voice within and *following* its direction. This requires the development of a persistent faith in your Higher Power, and according to the highest wisdom of many spiritual masters, it's clearly worth it.

The faith of which I speak has healing power, according to some fascinating medical research. More than 150 articles have been published by Harvard Medical School and elsewhere that show how belief can help you triumph over disease. Similar to the discussion of sangat in the last chapter, this research shows once more that spiritual living is indeed good for your health and longevity.

Recently, the prestigious *Journal of the American Medical Association* published an article showcasing evidence that faith and spiritual living have a positive effect in helping cure drug and alcohol abuse, emotional illness, chronic pain, and heart disease, as well as in improving general health. Most dramatically, other studies show that these

81

qualities may be as important as diet and exercise in helping you live a long life.

It's faith in God and His message heard in your soul that also takes you through the journey from the darkness of materiality (including disease and aging) to the light of the Divine. But remember: This isn't *blind* faith that just believes without any reason or experience. As your ability to hear the voice within grows and grows, your belief expands. Blind faith becomes obsolete because you have something greater: the experience of discovering the ultimate reality for which you've been searching—the God within yourself.

When you achieve this inner knowing, which is available to everyone, your feeling of exultation is difficult to describe. This state of spiritual development brings tremendous happiness, deep intuition, and tremendous self-worth.

It's interesting to note that as you surrender your ego and unconditionally accept the will of God as you understand it—and then implicitly act in accordance with it—you discover a level of serenity that you never knew existed, and you understand more fully the idea of seva, or selfless service. After you experience the Ultimate Being within your heart and soul, you'll often want to be a teacher yourself, for you'll find great pleasure in guiding others to the attainment of the "real" within themselves. Such is the power of the awakened soul to foster well-being in yourself and the world. Listening, you are forever in bliss.

Meditations on the Path

Communication is going on inside you all the time. Even when you verbalize and your ears hear it, it doesn't make any sense if your brain doesn't process it. If you don't understand yourself, you haven't developed the ability to listen to yourself, and when you listen for the voice of God, you're actually listening to *your* true self—for this is the only conscious voice that you have deep within you. It's a good habit to develop the capacity to listen to yourself whenever you're confronted with any challenges by saying in meditation, "I must listen to myself."

Listening Meditation

Here is a simple, yet powerful, meditation to help you tune in to your inner voice:

- **Posture:** Sit in a comfortable meditative posture in "easy pose" (see page 47) on the floor or in a chair. Keep your back straight, and be positive.

- **Focus:** Try to hear your inner voice, and close your eyes.

- **Mudra:** Cup your hands and place them over your ears. Stretch your thumbs out so that they come under your jawbone.

- **Mantra:** Inhale through your nose and begin singing softly in your own tune: "God and me, me and God, are one." Let your breath come naturally, but make it nice and deep.

- **Time:** Continue for 11 minutes.

- **To finish:** Inhale through your nose, hold your breath, and press your ears as hard as you can. Exhale, and then repeat one more time. Next, inhale deeply again, hold your breath, and keeping your hands over your ears, rock your body from side to side two to three times. Exhale and relax.

LISTENING MEDITATION

Comments: This is *simran,* chanting with the power of the breath, or *prana.* When you chant this mantra with prana, it will complete your communication with yourself. Your inner being will start talking to you, and you'll sit in ecstasy.

Stories on the Path:
She Is a Gift to You from God

At the outset of this book I asked if you thought God might talk to you. This is a good time to revisit that question. Do you believe in an inner voice, and do you think it represents your Higher Power? Please take a few minutes to think about it. . . .

I venture to say that if you've had the experience of hearing an inner voice, your answer was a resounding, "Yes!" If you've never had the experience, you may still be wondering if it's possible. (Of course, we're not talking about insanity here. We all know that people who are psychotic *do* hear voices, but obviously that's not what we're discussing.)

As you know by now, on a few occasions I've had the blessing of having God speak to me. In addition to the stories I've already shared, let me tell you about another time when I've actually had a higher calling.

Like many people, I made a mistake the first time around, and unfortunately my first marriage ended in divorce. Afterward, I had a relationship with a very lovely woman. Although we were close, it was clear to me that she and I were not going to be together forever, so we broke up. Subsequently, I felt terrible, because I really missed her a lot, so I decided that I'd try to win her back—which seemed like a pretty daunting task under the circumstances.

One morning I got up to meditate, and as I began, a powerful deep voice echoed in my mind: *She is not your destiny.* That got my attention, especially since on some level I knew that it was true. Not wanting to accept this reality, however, I told the voice, "Oh yeah, watch this!"

Then I began the long journey of trying to resume that relationship. I put a lot of energy into getting back together with her, and we did actually reunite—but it didn't last long. God was right: It just wasn't meant to be.

Although I had a few false starts after that, I essentially remained unattached and didn't enter into another serious relationship. I spent a fair amount of time alone in meditation.

One day about four years after the time I'd last heard my inner voice, I awoke early, as I usually do, to begin my sadhana. I began by chanting the mantra "Ong Namo Guru Dev Namo" (which means "I bow before my highest consciousness").

As I said a few silent affirmations and prayers, I realized that on this day my thoughts weren't my own, and as I entered into a pleasant, timeless state of being, an image appeared in my mind. I saw a vessel containing pure white milk shatter on a flat black surface. It was then swept away by a large, but otherwise ordinary, household broom—only to be replaced by a beautiful silver chalice as the following words echoed in my mind: *You have the most beautiful, perfect woman in the world for you now.*

This sequence repeated itself three more times before it stopped, and I continued with my practice of kundalini yoga and meditation. But the next morning it happened again, and the following day as well. Shortly thereafter I received a call from my spiritual teacher's secretary, who said that the yogi wanted me to come to New Mexico as soon as possible. When I asked why, he answered, "To meet your future wife."

The inner voice was right, because I did go and meet the woman who, two months later, became my wife. That was close to 13 years ago, and we're still very happy. We have a great relationship with a strong spiritual foundation.

On the day of our marriage, I remember Yogi Bhajan coming to be with my wife and me. We all seemed to meld together as he put his arms around both of us in a strong embrace. I heard him say in my ear, so perhaps only I could hear, "She is a gift to you from God."

In order to truly discover all your inborn gifts and live a life of exhilaration, you have to drop the obstacles that keep you stuck in doubt and pain. To do that requires you to not only listen and agree, but also to release some of your more negative habits. We'll explore how to do just that in the next chapter.

CHAPTER SIX

The Third New Golden Rule:
Dissolve Your Blocks

In this chapter, we'll look at the different aspects of the third New Golden Rule through the experience of a man who made the long journey of personal growth with the help of his spiritual teacher, and by following the previous two principles. As you read, think about how this story and the other examples apply to your own path.

Stories on the Path: At the Feet of the Master

Alexander wasn't a happy man. At age 42, he had a successful medical practice, a lovely wife, and a nice family, but something was gnawing at his soul. He wanted to live a more spiritual lifestyle, but felt that something was hindering him—he just couldn't figure out what it was.

Ten years earlier he'd begun practicing yoga and meditation, and he had the great blessing of meeting a living spiritual master who became his teacher. One day the frustrated doctor decided that he'd present his problem to his spiritual teacher, so he sent an e-mail to the master's secretary and was notified that he had an appointment at 2 P.M. the following Saturday.

The day came, and Alex wore a pair of white pants and a white shirt for the meeting. The color white is often worn by many advanced spiritual students, for it symbolizes purity and contains all the colors of the rainbow rolled into one. It's also the color of a very healthy human aura and signifies a connection to all beings. Out of respect for the holiness of the master, Alex also wrapped a white turban-like cloth around his head. (As you may know, many religious and highly spiritual people wear a head covering as a reminder to be mindful in each thought, word, and action that God is everywhere.)

After traveling quite a distance, first by plane and then by car, Alex arrived at his teacher's estate. He was shown into the living room, where he was to rest until it was his turn to see the master. As he absorbed the rarefied atmosphere, he was given a cup of tea and some food to eat.

It felt kind of strange and almost surreal being there. The energy was certainly different . . . as if time had slowed down. Alex felt stimulated and excited, but also deeply calm, as he relaxed into his surroundings.

After sitting down on a comfortable couch, a wonderful new sensation began to envelop him. It felt like instant, effortless meditation, and he found himself automatically rolling his eyes up slightly, as if looking into his head. From his medical background, he knew that this movement was stimulating his pituitary gland, one of the most important master glands in the brain. The chemicals his pituitary was releasing from this movement were sure to change him on a physical, mental, and emotional level; and he felt his molecules rearranging themselves as if he were being transformed into a new person. (Later, when describing this feeling to his wife, he would use the word *rejuvenating:* He felt refreshed and renewed.)

Sitting there in this state, Alex sensed his metabolism accelerating and his vision becoming sharp and clear. *I haven't even seen the master yet and look how high I'm getting,* he mused.

After a few moments, his focus returned to the present. *This place is gorgeous,* Alex thought as he took in his surroundings a little more carefully. Beautiful, bright Oriental rugs of all colors, especially reds and blues, covered the floor. He knew that they were of the highest quality—and so was everything else in the room. He noticed the deep comfortable chairs, ivory statues, and ornate and mystical tapestries and paintings that adorned the walls of the master's home. The effect was rich and elegant, yet otherworldly. Seeing it all reminded Alex of his teacher's history. . . .

The master came from a long lineage of spiritual leaders. When he was just three years old, his grandfather—an acknowledged saint—began taking him to all the holiest shrines in his native India. He began studying yoga at age six . . . and his first teacher was a direct descendant of Genghis Khan.

At the tender age of 16, his teacher proclaimed him a master—but that was only the beginning. While other yogis went off to live in the mountains in order to withdraw from society, the master's master taught him how to use his abilities to excel in the world. This is called practicing the spiritual discipline of a *house-holder:* one who functions in the world but isn't distracted by it.

He went to school and earned a master's degree in economics and a Ph.D. in the psychology of communication. In addition, he was a decorated military man, rising in the ranks of national service to become head of the entire customs agency in his native country.

The master was also a physically imposing man. While most Indian yogis were slight, he was strong, stood well over six feet tall, and was close to 220 pounds. His personal development kept increasing as well, and in his 20s, he married and had three children.

When the master was in his early 30s and at the height of his yogic powers, he felt that it was time for him to shed his remaining ego and become a true man of God. So every evening at midnight, he traveled some distance to the Golden Temple in Amritsar, India, and with a group of around 50 others, helped clean the marble floors on his hands and knees. This is considered a great seva (or selfless service) in that particular part of the world—and a great privilege as well.

[**Note from Dr. Dharma:** As you probably recall from my own experience described previously, the Golden Temple is a marvelous shrine where people from all over the world come on a spiritual pilgrimage to meditate, pray, and clear their karmas.]

And so it was that after three and a half years of this practice, the master was fully enlightened. It was this experience that made the him a humble servant of humankind.

A few years later, he heard about an exceptional yogi who lived in the mountains. Apparently this man knew a powerful kriya (or meditation exercise) that worked on many known and unknown levels of the body, mind, and spirit. The master—who, of course, was by now a renowned yogi himself—trudged into the mountains to try to see the other fellow and learn the special meditation.

But the other yogi refused to see him right away. First he required his visitor to bring him a carrot pudding, so the master went around to the shops in town and bought all the available yogurt to use in the pudding. Then every morning at dawn, at the conclusion of his sadhana, the master walked barefoot up the side of the mountain until he reached the other yogi's cave. This continued for a week before he was granted the blessing of learning the kriya.

Later, at the age of 40, he arrived in the United States with only $35 in his pocket and set about training teachers and building a worldwide network of students. Being a superb businessman, he started from scratch and built a legacy of what he called *conscious businesses*. These many enterprises (both for-profit and nonprofit) were very successful and paved the way for the master to serve many people.

He was a living example of spiritual prosperity, allowing God to work through him—and that same $35 that he brought to America remains on his altar to this day.

Alex then thought back to the very first time he'd met his teacher more than a decade ago. He'd been working in the hospital when another spiritual student had called him and said, "The master's here—maybe you can get to meet him. Come right over!" Alex did, and had the first of many phenomenal experiences at the feet of the master.

As he approached the house where the master was staying that day so many years ago, he felt a great wave of excitement and curiosity come over him. *After all,* he told himself, *it's not every day that you get to meet a true yoga master.*

His hopes were short-lived, however. As he approached the place, he saw so many cars out front and so many people milling about that he thought it would be impossible to meet the great man.

But then a remarkable thing happened: As he began going toward the front door, he felt a wave of energy change his direction and push him around toward the back entrance. The closer he got to the house, the more this current pulled him forward, and then he was inside—but there were so many others around that all he could see was a mass of bodies. Miraculously, this ocean of people simply parted, and he was once more propelled forward by an unseen hand. *This is how Moses must have felt parting the Red Sea,* Alex had thought.

Before he could think another thought, he was standing right in front of the master, who looked at him and asked in a deep booming voice, "So tell me, doctor, how much money do you make?"

"$150,000," replied Alex. The master said nothing. He simply lay back on the couch and went to sleep. And at that moment, Alex went into an automatic deep meditative state. Although he never fully understood what had happened back then—or why the master had asked him that particular question—he *did* realize that he'd met someone unique and very real. He also knew that he'd found his spiritual teacher.

Now the feeling that he had here today, ten years later, was very similar to the depth of the total relaxation he'd felt back then.

"He'll see you now." Alex was brought back to the present by the master's secretary, who'd silently entered the room.

The doctor got up and entered a long corridor on the way to the master's quarters—only this wasn't any ordinary hallway: On the walls were long swords and around 150 true fighting knives (called *kirpans*), according to Alex's fast but accurate count. There were also photos of other obviously enlightened men, including the master's own personal spiritual guide, Guru Ram Das.

Guru Ram Das was actually the man who began building the Golden Temple more than 500 years ago (it was completed by his son, Guru Arjan). Although Guru Ram Das was well recognized as a powerful leader, saint, and healer, he was also very humble. It's said that he'd disguise himself as a peasant and go to the gates of the city every night, where he used his long beard to clean the feet of those who were coming to bow their heads at the holy site. When asked why he did this, Guru Ram Das said he wanted to be "the dust of the saint's feet."

Alex felt as if he were going through the hallway of a great warrior, yet he knew that the master was a most loving and peaceful man, and he wondered how that apparent discrepancy could ever be understood. (Later, however, when he had a chance to think about it, he realized that one can be peaceful and loving and still be strong. In fact, as you'll soon discover, Alex came to know firsthand that it's only love that can reduce mental and spiritual poisons such as hate, anger, fear, and resentment.)

At that moment, Alex was swept along by a wave of energy through the hallway of a saint-soldier into what almost seemed to be another dimension. He came out on the other side of this experience to be greeted once again by the master's booming voice laced with infectious laughter: "Hey, doctor, how are you?"

Holy gammoly, Alex thought, *here we go again.* Just as it had been the first time they met, Alex could feel the vitality jumping off the master's body, along with a peaceful calm radiating from his mind.

"What I can do for you?" the master asked.

"Sir," Alex began, "how far do I have to travel to know God and find spiritual bliss?"

The great man turned to him and looked through Alex's eyes, deep into his soul, and the student could feel his power. The master then bent down with love and compassion welling up in his luminous dark eyes and placed the tip of his little finger on Alex's navel point. He then spread his fingers wide enough to put his thumb on Alex's heart.

"Just this far, my son," he said. "The path seems short, but you must have great courage to walk it. Along the way you'll be confronted by three great obstacles."

"Please tell me what they are, sir," Alex replied.

"They are anger, grief, and fear."

"What can I do?" he asked.

"Develop the courage and consciousness to overcome these obstacles, my son. Make this journey into your own heart," the master counseled. "Start with forgiveness and see where it leads."

Before he knew it, Alex was out of the room and then had left his teacher's quarters. *Did this really happen?* he wondered, and his inner voice replied, *Oh yes, it did, Alex—and you'd better listen.*

Understanding Obstacles

The three great obstacles that the master told Alex he had to confront—anger, grief, and fear—are all hindrances to spiritual growth because they keep you stuck in the lower realms of emotional experience. As long as you remain trapped by these base emotions, it's difficult to transform yourself spiritually. But when you're able to raise your energy to the level of your heart, as the master suggested, you're then open to higher knowledge and experiences.

A strong and consistent spiritual practice (the initial principle of the first New Golden Rule) helps you develop love, compassion, intuition, and connection. And when you open up your higher centers through spiritual living, you realize the universal cosmic energy as the determining factor in your life . . . and then you're in bliss.

The First Blocks: Anger and Depression

Alex knew very well that he needed to work on forgiveness, but he was glad to hear the master confirm it. For in spite of all the obvious blessings in his life, there was definitely one thing that kept irritating him like a burr under a saddle: Alex had a very poor relationship with his mother, and he carried around a lot of anger and resentment toward her. This was one thing that he couldn't seem to resolve in his mind, and as he got older, it was more and more of a burden.

Very often you can understand something intellectually but still have difficulty releasing your negative energy, and that's the way it was with Alex. On some level he knew that his mother had tried her best to do the right thing for him, but that didn't make it any easier to forgive her for all the pain he felt she'd caused him.

When Alex was only five, his parents divorced, and he and his mother moved away to a different state. He never saw his father after that and was raised by his mother, who often said that she had to be both a mother and a father to him. Alex saw this as the source of his anger, for in his mind, her desire to be his father robbed him of the warmth of a mother's love. In essence, he felt he had almost no parental support.

Because she thought she had to be a father, his mother was rough with Alex, often yelling at and being critical of him. What he needed during those times of denigration, however, was a hug and a mother's love. As he thought back, he recalled how he'd wall himself off from the situation to try to escape the pain of the moment. Even now, the deep-seated memory of the horrible combination of rage and helplessness that he felt back then was almost overwhelming. Clearly these experiences had left a nearly indelible mark on his psyche.

As I alluded to earlier in this book, many people have the perception that they weren't taken care of properly as a child. Perhaps they weren't loved enough, or like Alex, they had the subtle perception of not being nurtured enough. According to the ancient laws of Eastern medicine, which have been around since the dawn of time, this perception of a lack of being nurtured may lead to a number of physical, emotional—and yes, even spiritual—deficiencies.

Alex was a bit unusual in this regard because his main problem was anger. But as the master saw, he also needed to work on his grief (the loss of not having a proper home) and his fear of letting go so that he could move on to be as spiritual as he knew he wanted to be. Alex was out of the ordinary because people who see themselves as not being nurtured usually suffer from depression, not anger. In fact, those who aren't nurtured as children may suffer from what I call "cold depression," which is a very deep pain and is quite difficult to defrost, even if the patient is treated with talk therapy, antidepressant medication such as Prozac, or a combination of the two.

Deep, cold, frozen depression is the usual manifestation of the perception of not being nurtured as a child, and it's an epidemic running rampant in our society among the so-called baby-boom generation. If you've ever known someone like this, then perhaps you recall that when they weren't depressed, they exhibited anger. People who have this perception, like Alex, may flip-flop back and forth between anger and depression. That's why this problem is so difficult to treat with conventional medicine: No drug can touch it completely.

Ancient healers were tuned in to this phenomenon and were the first to consider proper nurturance a biological imperative. In fact, the ancients also recognized that a mother's emotional state during pregnancy determined the quality, nature, character, capacity, size, and function of her infant's neurological system. For this reason, they suggested that an expectant mother meditate, chant, pray, and listen to sacred hymns daily throughout her pregnancy. The saints, sages, and yogis of India through the ages have also taught that continued emotional well-being within the family is crucial for a child's development of many of our most precious human virtues. Creativity, love, and proper social adaptation are among those vital traits.

These ideas of the enlightened healers have now been subject to study by medical scientists. More than 50 years ago, scholars at Harvard Medical School looked at differences in the emotional quality of infancy and childhood and the effect these stages had on future mental and physical health. They found that those children who said that they didn't feel nurtured, loved, or supported by their parents had close to four times as much difficulty with their health later in life.

Alex was familiar with this research and knew that his emotional deprivation in his formative years was probably responsible for some of his psychological difficulties as an adult. He'd more or less worked through his tendency toward depression because for the past ten years, he'd been doing a strong and consistent sadhana. It's almost impossible to remain depressed if you do a good spiritual practice every day, since you dramatically change your brain chemicals for the better. A vigorous yoga set and nice, deep meditation produce an abundant amount of the natural antidepressants serotonin, norepinephrine, and dopamine. So Alex wasn't depressed—but he was definitely angry, especially at his mother.

Beginning to Let Go . . . Before It's Too Late

Okay, Alex told himself one afternoon while taking a walk, *I know all this stuff, but it doesn't make it any easier. I can't seem to forgive her—and I'm not sure I want to.*

He was stuck with his emotions and was also attached to them (we'll look at attachment later in this chapter). He felt that he had good reason to be angry—after all, his problems with this relationship hadn't ended with childhood. If they had, perhaps it would have been easier for him to let go. Alex thought back over his adult years and all the trouble with his mother. Even his wife had commented that his mother didn't treat him very well, and that she was always trying to get in a barb or a criticism. In fact, it made his wife uncomfortable to be around her.

Anger isn't a pleasant emotion. It may be normal at times, but it isn't necessarily natural—or healthy—to hold on to it year after year, planning retribution and revenge. If someone does something that upsets you, it's best to express your feelings and move on. An appropriate response might be: "When you did such and such, I felt angry."

I'm not saying that you still have to have a relationship with that person, because sometimes it's better to take care of or protect yourself by leaving a situation or relationship— and that's especially true if there's physical danger or emotional abuse involved. But the worst thing that you can do is not express your feelings and hold on to your resentment.

Anger is an emotion that can damage your health—and even kill you. The terrible stress hormones that your glands secrete into your blood at these times (such as adrenaline and cortisol) may cause heart disease, high blood pressure, and perhaps even cancer. Therefore, carrying around a toxic load of resentment, conflict, or bitterness is highly detrimental to your system and causes increased wear and tear on your body, which can lead to accelerated aging. Cortisol in particular has a number of horrible effects on the brain that have been scientifically proven to lead to memory loss.

I know it's difficult to release these emotions because I've been there myself. But if you can accept the insights I'm sharing with you, I believe that you will absolutely dissolve this block to bliss.

Positive Healing Messages

Forgiveness, on the other hand, is a positive emotion. It changes your cell structure for the better because it can actually cause the release of healing chemicals into your bloodstream. I call the effects of these good chemicals "positive healing messages," because they go all the way down to the level of your cells. Once these substances get there, they can create what doctors and scientists call "second and third messengers," which are compounds that tell your genes what to do. They can allow your DNA to express their genetic code by manufacturing various peptides and compounds that have a healing effect on your body, such as reducing inflammation or enhancing your immune function.

But physical health isn't the main incentive to learn how to let go. The real reason that I suggest you work on forgiveness is because it will take you on a wonderful journey toward understanding life and bring you closer to your Higher Self. Moreover, always remember that you'll get back what you give. So learn to forgive, and see what beauty and love return to you.

As anyone who has ever tried it can tell you, forgiveness is often not an easy task, and it may take years. This usually entails an important internal process that can extend for a very long time, as it did in Alex's case. In other words, it may not occur automatically, and it certainly doesn't happen overnight. But when you do forgive—even just a little bit—it feels as if a heavy load has been lifted off your back.

Alex Forgives

Although learning to forgive usually takes quite some time, the process *can* be accelerated, and the master's insights certainly moved Alex forward. Once he began to travel down the road to forgiveness, he allowed the

Universe to work its miracles on him. . . .

One afternoon, Alex was driving in his car while listening to a talk-radio station. The guest that day happened to be a well-known self-help author and speaker whose name he recognized (he thought he might have seen her on *Oprah*). Out of what appeared to be the clear blue sky, the author began speaking about forgiveness, and it seemed as if she was speaking directly to Alex.

"Forgive," she said. "Especially forgive your mother."

That definitely got his attention, because it was exactly what he was thinking about at that moment, and had been pondering for such a long time. Alex finally surrendered: *Okay, I hereby forgive her.*

That night as he was sleeping, the phone rang. It was the hospital where Alex worked—the floor where seriously ill elderly patients were taken. "Doctor," the nurse said, "I'm afraid you need to come to the hospital right away."

"What's wrong?" Alex asked. "I don't think I'm on call this evening."

"No," the nurse replied, "but your mother is here, and she's not expected to live."

Unbelievable! Alex thought as he hung up the phone. *The day that I forgive her, she has to die. Here's another thing to be angry about—she always has to have the last word.*

He drove as fast as he could to the hospital and went immediately to his mother's room. Her doctor was there, and after checking all the monitors, she took Alex out into the hallway. "Your mom came in this evening, and it seems she's gone into heart failure," she said.

"Well, what are you doing to treat her?" Alex asked.

"Not much," was the reply. "After all, she's 86 years old, and it's probably not cost-effective to put her in the ICU."

"But at least we can do the basics," Alex insisted. "Why haven't you even gotten an x-ray or a blood-gas analysis? Any medical student would know what to do in this case!"

Alex took over his mother's care right then and there. Staying at the hospital, he had all the proper procedures done, and even had to perform one of the more difficult blood tests himself because the technician couldn't hit the artery. He then strongly suggested that his mother be placed on oxygen and given her heart medicine. He couldn't get her transferred into the intensive care unit, so he stayed in her room most of the night in order to make sure that everything was done correctly.

His mother survived that night in the hospital, and she was almost as good as new when she was discharged five days later. Alex had consciously forgiven her and was then able to save her life. Such is the power of spiritual forgiveness.

I'd like to be able to tell you that things were perfect between mother and son after that, but they weren't. At least Alex was able to understand that his mother had always tried the best she could, and as she aged and became ill, she didn't have the consciousness to address the problems they faced.

So Alex did the inner work of changing himself because he knew that he couldn't change his mother. When they were together, he no longer played into her negativity and was able to simply be with her. He also prayed for her every day during his morning sadhana. Prayer is a very powerful tool to resolve resentment, and he felt it working.

When he forgave his mother and began praying for her,

he noticed his own stress and anger melting away. He never forgot the situations he'd endured, but he was able to rise above them. Not only did Alex forgive his mother, but he also began to forgive his past—and even himself.

The ultimate lesson he learned from this experience is that all forgiveness begins with inner work and ends with having the courage to forgive yourself. The more you forgive yourself, the more you love and accept yourself, and this is healing in action.

Alex realized that he could never get rid of the pain of the past unless he began working to dissolve the blocks that kept him stuck in anguish: fear, anger, and grief. True, none of this was his fault, but in reality these situations aren't *anyone's* fault. They just are what they are.

In the end, he came to appreciate that this situation was given to his soul by God in order for him to grow and progress on his own spiritual path. Alex realized that it's the pressure on the coal that brings out the diamond within each person.

As you work on forgiving yourself and others and releasing your negative emotions, you'll become more self-accepting, optimistic, and peaceful. Aim to be like God and live a life of mercy, compassion, and forgiveness, for it will take you to bliss.

Is there someone you need to forgive? Perhaps you can begin now.

Another Block to Bliss: Grief

Like anger, grief is another obstacle that you may have to deal with on your quest to bring more spirit into your life and find bliss. Now, sometimes the direct cause of your grief may be quite obvious, such as the loss of a loved one. But at other times, the root of your emotion, or even the grief itself, may be beyond your awareness. For example, you may not realize that the symptoms of depression you're experiencing are related to the loss of a relationship you expected to work out but didn't, or to a job promotion you didn't receive.

Regardless of the cause, however, grief is about loss. Yet the problem isn't really the feeling itself, because grief is a normal emotion. The trouble occurs when you hold on to it, because this blocks your acceptance of the situation and prevents you from moving on to the next stage of your life.

In Chinese medicine, this lack of movement is called "stagnation," and is thought to be the cause of serious mental and physical illness. Movement, on the other hand, promotes health and enhances growth. At various times in this book, I've discussed the importance of being in the flow of life and the power of listening to your inner voice and accepting God's will for you. When you're able to do these things, you're also able to dissolve the obstacle to spiritual growth that we know as grief.

It's often hard to let go, especially of a loved one. But in reality, you aren't doing *anyone* any good, neither yourself nor the departed one, by holding on to grief. It's best to incorporate prayer for the soul of the person into your practice as part of your grief process.

I'm not just talking about death here, either—if you've experienced a relationship breakup, that can certainly be a major loss as well. In that case, grieve as much as you need to. But at some point (whenever it feels right for you), begin to let go and move on in your life by praying for the soul of the other person and realizing that if it had been meant to be, it would have happened.

Keep in mind that acceptance is to grief as forgiveness is to anger. Once you move back into the flow of life and accept what is, you'll find that you begin to open up physically, mentally, and spiritually. In a manner similar to the forgiveness process I described earlier, once you make peace with the way things are in the present moment, you draw the positive energy of the next stage of your life to you. As I also mentioned before, nature abhors a vacuum, so when you begin to accept and release, the Universe guides you to what's next in your life.

True acceptance will transform your life because it will take you one step further to the realization that God is all. So why not begin to let go right now, and let God do His job?

Fear and Faith

Now that we've discussed two very powerful emotions—anger and grief—and how you need to dissolve them, let's look at the third negative emotion that the master brought to Alex's attention: fear. We've all probably been affected by this obstacle in one way or another. This primal, motivating urge might even be the underlying cause of most crimes and destructive activities by individuals and nations.

While fear probably kept many of our ancestors alive through the ages, we don't need to make use of this primitive emotion today in the same way that we once did. And beyond that, we just don't need to be afraid as much as we are—there's simply too much anxiety among people today.

Evolving to a higher level of being involves dissolving

fear, as Moses, Abraham, Jesus, Buddha, Gandhi, and other great personalities throughout history have shown. Realizing this can help you on your journey to a higher spiritual consciousness, and you can begin by asking yourself, "Do I have a powerful fear that's affecting my life?"

Most apprehension is actually irrational and has no real cause—it's more like a dread of the unknown. The problem is that when you project fear, you manifest it, because what you dwell upon, you bring to fruition. Again, this is another example of the way the universe works: What you put out, you get back.

When you say, "Yes, but I'm afraid," the first question you must answer is, "Afraid of what? What *exactly* is it that I fear?" This is a difficult task because most people really aren't sure of the origins of their fear.

I'd been wondering about this myself one day as I was being driven to a presentation in downtown Mexico City. It became clear to me during that ride that all our worry boils down to the fear of death. After all, if you knew that you weren't going to pass away, then there really wouldn't be anything to fear.

Think back to Dana's story in Chapter 2 (see page 12) and the information we've gleaned about near-death experiences. Apparently there's nothing to fear about dying, except perhaps the unknown. People are insecure about it because they think that they don't know what's going to happen. Therefore, they're afraid. That's what this is based on—not knowing, or what I call the "fear of the unseen," because we don't know what's behind the veil.

The solution to dissolving this block is to end your relationship with it, which may be easier than you think. Once I was listening to a speaker discuss managing money, but his presentation wasn't that impressive, and I was losing interest.

Then he said something that really got my attention: He was talking about spending money and casually said that he didn't feel guilty about it. To this day, I remember the next few simple words he uttered, because they had a great impact on me: "I don't have a relationship with guilt." I thought, *Oh, really?* And I decided at that moment that I wouldn't have a relationship with guilt either.

Sometime later, as I was going through the process of dissolving my fear, I went back to that day in my mind and said to myself, *Well, if I don't have to have a relationship with guilt, then perhaps I don't have to have one with fear.*

Then the other side of my mind worried, *Oh, that's a tough one.*

I now realize that the dissolution of fear is so difficult because of what I mentioned above: We all have a subtle (and sometimes not-so-subtle) fear of death, the "final frontier" that symbolizes the end. But what if it *isn't?* What if the so-called end of our physical life is actually another beginning—a peaceful, easy, loving experience?

I believe Dana's story, and the information provided by the research on NDEs tells us that there's a living consciousness after we die. Beyond that, isn't our soul immortal? *It* never dies, does it? If so, then there's no such thing as death—there's only living in all its different forms. Therefore we're *all* living a life without death.

As a spiritual seeker, I know that you want to develop the image of the Divine within yourself. One of God's most admirable traits is that He is courageous. So be like Him, and have no fear.

Because your Source is the doer of all things and watches over you with love, protection, and grace, why not let go of your worries and have faith that He is taking care of all your needs? Leave your destiny in the hands of the ever-expanding universe rather than limiting yourself with fear. Learn to grow your faith and lean on your Higher Power; try to release your doubts, have patience, and watch all the best things come to you.

This negative emotion has another troubling effect as well: Sometimes you may not appreciate everything that you have because you're so involved in your relationship with fear. That's why I suggest that you take a few moments, perhaps now or during an evening period of reflection, to visualize or write down all the wonderful things that have come your way. This is a nice spiritual practice that yields many pleasant benefits, and I know it will help you begin to release your doubt and anxiety, whatever their causes.

Three More Blocks to Melt Away

There are other obstacles to spiritual growth in addition to anger, grief, and fear. They're all similar, however, in that they keep you stuck and attached to living from your ego—which, as you know by now, is the opposite of living from the depths of your soul. These other hassles are greed, pride, and attachment.

In essence, all your challenges on the path to greater awareness, regardless of what you call them, are simply one side of a two-sided coin—part of a polarity. Just about everything you can think of has an opposite: Rain has sunshine; up has down; in has out; and I'm sure you can come up with many others. Well, the chief blocks on your spiritual path also have their flip sides. For example, you've seen that anger has forgiveness, grief has acceptance and resolution, and fear has faith and courage.

There are interesting ways to consider the converse aspects of greed, pride, and attachment as well. I believe that if you can "change the channel" of your mind and examine these characteristics with a new point of view, you'll see how you can turn a negative into a positive.

Let's look at each concept individually to explain what I mean in detail.

Greed

Of course you already know the negative side to greed: It causes you to put an excessive focus on money or other material objects for their own sake. If you find yourself in the grip of this quality, you may cheat, lie, or steal without remorse, just to increase your net worth. Then you either spend it on yourself in one way or another, or hoard it. There's nothing wrong with spending money or saving for a rainy day, but if you discover that you're living in greed, you know that you're clearly out of balance when it comes to material possessions. You may realize that you just want more and more money—for money's sake alone.

On the other side of greed is generosity. You dissolve the negative when you earn wealth by your own means, education, or skills; and then instead of spending it furiously or hoarding it, you share it with others less fortunate than yourself. You can be "greedy" to give to others, to want time for meditation, or to serve humanity—these are manifestations of the good part of excessive desire, and I'm sure that you can think of many more generous acts to melt this block away.

Pride

Pride is an ego-based emotion that has you thinking that everything is about you, rather than recognizing that a Higher Power sets everything in motion. If you're out of balance in pride, it will be very difficult for you to develop compassion and love because they demand an open heart.

This challenge closes off your love—it's constricting and limiting—but luckily, it's also one of the easiest base emotions to release. Once you begin living on a higher spiritual plane, it's highly unlikely that you'll be stuck in pride, because as you listen to the voice within and agree with its direction (the second New Golden Rule), it becomes virtually impossible to think that you're the doer. Instead, you come to the rapid conclusion that it's the Unseen Force guiding us all that's orchestrating the music of your life.

Attachment

I actually think that *everything* is about attachment. Nothing in this world is permanent, but it's difficult to come to that realization. Many people are attached to their youth (even though it doesn't last forever), perhaps spending a lot of money on special creams or surgeries to try to recapture something that can never be regained. Some individuals may have their hair transplanted, their faces lifted, their eyes done, their breasts augmented or reduced, or their tummies tucked.

True beauty, however, comes <u>only</u> from the inside—from your shining soul.

You see, everything on this earthly plane is transient, including life itself—which is a bit like watching a movie: First you go into the theater and eat some popcorn; next you watch the show; and when it's over, you leave. Or perhaps you might consider our earthly experience similar to checking into a hotel: You stay awhile, you enjoy it, and then you check out. That's life.

Even though on some level you know that everything's changing, you may remain attached to what was. This traps you in the past and prevents you from living in the precious present. It also keeps you from properly considering the future. In other words, you're holding on to things, events, or people rather than letting go and watching life take its own natural rhythm; grasping and clinging rather than allowing events to unfold naturally. Yet how can you go through an open door if you're attached to trying to keep the previous one from closing?

This is a normal human quality—it's just not a mature trait of an evolved spiritual person living in bliss. Worse than that, excessive attachment leads to suffering, and in my experience, a great deal of it. So what can you do about it?

Well, the opposite of attachment is still . . . attachment—just not to your ego. The polarity of negative connections is positive ones. Be attached to bringing people pleasure instead of aggravation, and try not to suffocate others or yourself. Devote yourself to feeding the hungry and doing good. In these cases, your commitment will have value instead of causing pain to yourself or others.

So be attached to your spiritual energy first, and then observe everything else in your life fall into place. If you need things, they'll come to you, for as you become more aware of the power of positive attachments, you can watch your horizons expand and your environment prosper.

As Yogi Bhajan has said: "The best attachment is to be attached to your character and consciousness and move it through your 'intelligence.'" Remember, it's your actions that bring you closer to God or keep you far apart.

Meditations on the Path

As you witnessed with Alex, sometimes it takes a long time to release your anger and learn to forgive. Eliminating your anxiety and fear can also be a lengthy process, and quite often it takes years to learn to live in balance. That's why I'm including a few advanced meditations to help you dissolve these blocks to bliss. I don't want it to take a lifetime for you to get to where you need to be.

Sometimes you may want to go from Los Angeles to Miami, or New York to San Francisco. You have options when you travel—such as walking or taking a bus, train, or plane—but you usually choose the fastest method because you don't want to waste time. You want to get where you're going, physically *and* spiritually, and that's why these meditations are here. They're rapid-acting and precise, and will take you where you want to go quickly and safely.

Pick the meditation that you feel you relate to the most, and then practice it for 40 days without missing a day. Enjoy, and "keep up."

Meditation to Release Childhood Anger

*   **Posture:** Sit in a comfortable meditative posture in "easy pose" (see page 47) on the floor or in a

chair with your back straight. Stretch your arms out straight to the sides. There's no bend in the elbows.

- **Mudra:** With each hand, use your thumb to lock down your pinkie and ring fingers while you extend your index and middle fingers. Your palms face forward and your fingers point out to the sides.

- **Breath:** Open your lips slightly and inhale deeply by sucking air through your closed teeth. Exhale through your nose.

- **Time:** Continue for 11 minutes.

- **To Finish:** Inhale deeply through your mouth and hold your breath for ten seconds while you stretch your spine up and stretch your arms out to the sides. Now exhale. Repeat this sequence two more times.

MEDITATION TO RELEASE
CHILDHOOD ANGER

Comments: This meditation will give you subtle powers—it will change you inside and out. The exercise can be done either in the morning or in the evening. If you choose the evening, the next morning you'll find that your outlook on life has changed for the better.

Meditation to Conquer Inner Anger

*   **Posture:** Sit in a comfortable meditative posture in "easy pose" (see page 47) on the floor or in a chair with your back straight. Stretch your arms out straight to the sides with no bend in your elbows. Your index fingers point up, and your thumb locks down your other fingers. Your index fingers need to be stiff and straight.

*   **Focus:** Close your eyes and concentrate on your spine.

*   **Breath:** Roll your tongue into a U shape. Open your mouth and let your tongue come out slightly, and then inhale through your open mouth so that the air is felt on your tongue. This is known as *sitali* breath. Exhale through your nose.

*   **Time:** Continue for 11 minutes.

*   **To finish:** Inhale deeply through your mouth; hold your breath for ten seconds while you stretch your arms out to the sides as far as possible, then exhale. Repeat this sequence two more times.

MEDITATION TO
CONQUER INNER ANGER

Comments: This meditation can be done either in the morning or the evening. If you do this meditation 11 minutes a day for 40 days, your entire life will change because you'll have released so much negativity.

Occasionally, you may find that it hurts to do this exercise. That's a good thing, and it means that now is the time to keep going so that your brain will release its endorphins (which, as you probably know, are your body's own morphine). Then when you breathe the sitali breath, it will kill your innermost anger—but you have to get angry with the pain. The more you hurt, the angrier you'll be; the more upset you are, the more you'll breathe; and the more you breathe, the less anger you'll have. It's a great meditation.

Meditation to Help Forgiveness by Relieving Stress and Resolving Issues from the Past

- **Posture:** Sit in a comfortable meditative posture in "easy pose" (see page 47) on the floor or in a chair with your back straight.

- **Mudra:** Bring your hands to the center of your chest with the tips of your thumbs touching each other, and each fingertip touching the corresponding finger of your opposite hand. There's a space between your palms, and your fingertips are pointing upwards.

- **Focus:** Look at the tip of your nose.

- **Breath:** All breathing in this meditation is done through the nose. Complete four breaths per minute in the following way: Inhale for five seconds, hold for five seconds, and exhale for five seconds.

- **Time:** Continue for 11 minutes.

- **To Finish:** Inhale deeply and hold your breath for ten seconds, then exhale. Repeat two more times.

MEDITATION TO HELP FORGIVENESS
BY RELIEVING STRESS AND
RESOLVING ISSUES FROM THE PAST

Relaxing Buddha Meditation to Eliminate Fear

This is a very calming meditation that will help you dissolve fear in just 11 minutes.

- **Posture:** Sit in a comfortable meditative posture in "easy pose" (see page 47) on the floor or in a chair.

- **Mudra:** Your right elbow is bent and resting on your right knee. Lean your right cheekbone on the palm of your right hand with your fingers loosely covering the right half of your forehead.

- **Focus:** Close your eyes and relax as deeply as you can. This posture will put pressure on your liver, so just release any tension and let your body adjust to it. Breathe long and deep through the nose. You may play any type of very relaxing music.

- **To Finish:** Inhale for 20 seconds through your nose, hold your breath for 20 seconds, and then exhale through your nose for 20 seconds. Continue through two more cycles. (If you can't initially do such long intervals, just do the best you can do. For example, try five seconds at first, and work your way up.) Then inhale deeply and let all your tension go.

RELAXING BUDDHA
MEDITATION TO
ELIMINATE FEAR

Comments: Please relax further by listening to your favorite music for as long as you can after completing this meditation.

⸺ ᎒᎒ ⸺

You're now ready to reach for the zenith of spiritual bliss. The fourth New Golden Rule is the epitome of grace, although it may at first seem like a challenge that's just beyond your grasp. I want to assure you that having come this far, you are indeed prepared to take the next step, which we'll explore in the next chapter.

⸺ ᎒᎒ ⸺

CHAPTER SEVEN

The Fourth New Golden Rule:
See the Other Person
As Yourself

The fourth New Golden Rule is to see the other person as yourself. When you're able to do so, then you're able to see that others are souls who carry a spark of the Divine inside, just as you do. Begin working with this idea by just trying to keep it in mind as you go through the busy hours of your day.

A well-known early 20th-century Jewish philosopher, Emmanuel Levinas, described this principle as "seeing the Other in the other." Being a student of the Old Testament, he was referring to the Hebrew notion of "Betzelem Elohim," as stated in Genesis, which means "created in the image of God." Each person's soul, which was given to them by the Creator, is pure and without defects. So when you view others as yourself, you witness their gift from God.

Having been his student for so many years, I love Yogi Bhajan's succinct motto, which marvelously sums up the fourth New Golden Rule: "If you can't see God in all, then you can't see God at all."

When you follow this principle, your interactions occur on a much more loving, intimate, and unified level; and in this simple act, bliss and enlightenment become possible. Reaching the stage of spiritual development where you remember the fourth New Golden Rule means that you've achieved an elevated state of being where you're able to easily surrender to the will of your Higher Power, which isn't defeat, but a clear-cut victory for your soul on your journey of self-development.

We Are All Divine

While each one of us is certainly unique, we have many more similarities than differences. The myth of separation from each other is a by-product of our egocentric minds, for we're all one—and research results from the white-hot cutting edge of physics, genetics, and theology all agree with this. The big bang theory, for example, states that the Universe (and hence all life), began when a mass of concentrated energy reached a certain intensity and exploded—which means that we're all derived from that same initial force.

The theory of evolution leads to the idea that all humanity descends from the same ancestral lineage, while strict Biblical interpretation also tells us that we all have similar roots: Adam and Eve. Finally, modern genetic thought assures us that there's very little difference between the DNA makeup of one human being and another. We all apparently come from one Creator, and we're all brothers and sisters in the Divine.

Consistently looking beyond a person's physical form and personality—and thus relating to others as souls—develops the positive personality characteristics of hope, optimism, and love to a high degree. These are important traits that are scientifically proven to provide an excellent foundation for effective living as they enhance well-being and increase meaning in your life. And as I've mentioned at various times throughout this book, having a sense of purpose is one of the most significant determinants of happiness—and something that following the New Golden Rules will help you achieve.

Manifesting the Challenge

Sociological studies have shown that people who know that they're in the last stage of their life always explore the nature of meaning. Those who are most content at that point have been able to pinpoint a hearty relationship with their soul as one of their main sources of meaning in their life. Peace of mind at any time of life, especially at the end, is extraordinarily remarkable, but please recall that the purpose of living these four principles is to discover bliss *now,* wherever you are, rather than waiting for your final days.

Research over the past 15 years has not only demonstrated the health benefits of optimism, but also that pessimists can be taught the techniques of positive thinking. Adults and children who acquire these skills have less anxiety and depression and fewer stress-related disorders than those who remain pessimistic, sarcastic, or scornful. The hope, optimism, and love that you develop in your being from seeing the One in all not only improves your own outlook on life, it also raises the consciousness of others: Your attitude is infectious and can influence other people for the better by making them happier.

When you begin to see other people as souls, you understand the goodness in them. The ability to notice others' faults, but choosing to overlook them and relate to the Divine within, brings you another step closer to bliss.

The Buddha taught this lesson in an extremely interesting way. He recommended that if you want to relate to a person on a higher level, you should visualize them as a speck of dust or a bunch of bones. It's certainly a pragmatic idea, because at some point in time we'll all be either one or both of these two things. I'd like to suggest to you, however, that it may be more pleasant to imagine that you're speaking or relating to the soul of others while they're living, breathing entities in the here-and-now.

My wife, Kirti, practices this in a gentle way. When she encounters someone acting negatively, her thought process may be as follows: *This person is a human just like me. Maybe they're tired, and that's why they're being grumpy.*

Kirti told me that she mentally lists all the possible things that might have happened to make the individual out of balance, and then she added, "Actually, the way I do it is to remember all the possible things that may have happened to *me* at one time or another to make me act unpleasant. Then I think that maybe one of these things happened to this other person. This automatically helps make my irritability or impatience evaporate."

Seeing beyond outer appearances makes it easier to see

the Higher Power in each person . . . and then perceive the God in everything, which is the highest spiritual attribute you can have.

Sharing Our Peace

Transcending the superficial to take the spiritual view helps you learn to actually ignore most of the negative aspects of other people. Moreover, seeing their virtue (as opposed to their faults) strengthens your own higher qualities, and your consciousness changes for the better. Your communication will be clearer, calmer, and much more open, because you'll feel a deep inner peace, which will radiate freely outward to touch everyone around you. In this way, you're doing your part to spread peace and light to all.

When we're all able to come to the point where we manifest this fourth principle, we may be able to end some of the most challenging social issues that we face in our world today, such as racism. In addition, when we're able to see everybody as having the same value—and therefore perhaps enjoy more diplomatic communication—we may finally be able to bring peace to the world.

With all our modern-day hustle and bustle, it's quite challenging to see or feel God *anywhere* sometimes, let alone see Him *everywhere* and in everyone. But once you're living the first three New Golden Rules and have had the experience of being in bliss, you'll naturally begin to see the One everywhere—and then you'll be happier than you ever thought possible. What will really get your attention, though, will be how smoothly your life goes once you see the spark of the Divine in every home and heart.

Surrendering Judgment

Some people have a certain belief that's along these lines: "Oh, this good thing that happened is God," or "Thank God for this or that." I agree that what we perceive as the One Source's positive blessings can be immeasurable, but the so-called negative things that happen are also Divine. How can it be any other way if God is all?

I remember that my grandmother used to say, "Into every life some rain must fall." I know that sometimes it feels as if a hurricane is blowing right down on you, but if God is all and the doer of everything, then the turmoil that comes down into your life must also be a gift from Him.

At first this may be a difficult concept to grasp, but you'll come to understand it over time. Remember: Realizing that God's will is everything and learning to live in that flow will lead you to bliss. Your Higher Power alone knows your destiny and gives to you accordingly. What may at first appear to be good may later turn out to be the opposite, while what you thought was terrible may actually be for the best. Or you may never know why something happens . . . but you can be sure that it's all God's will for you.

To make the process easier to understand, perhaps you can think back on an event in your life that started out being awful but ended up actually being something positive.

Learning to Grow

We've been programmed to interpret "negative" events as possible punishment for our sins, or we may feel that we're unworthy of success—or any number of other guilt-based concepts. Yet if we can view these experiences as opportunities for personal and spiritual growth, and if we can understand that the cosmos itself is continuing to expand, then acceptance and understanding—rather than judgment or reckoning—may be easier to achieve.

It's the nature of the Universe, and therefore of all things in it (including us humans), to be part of a cycle of continual contraction and expansion. In order for things to grow, it takes a resisting force to help generate the energy required to expand.

Birth itself is a prime example of this phenomenon. If you've ever had a baby or witnessed one being born, then I'm sure you know what I mean. First, a mother must push to expel the child; and the fetus must work as well, moving its way toward the light and that first, precious breath. It's often painful, difficult work for both mother and baby. The process is both life-giving and life-threatening—unstoppable and undeniable.

In the traditions of the East, all things—from rocks to trees to water to human beings—are considered to have a life-force energy in them, with the whole Universe alive and vibrating. Everything is growing on one level or another, including you as an individual. In order to evolve, you must face challenges that take you beyond the perception of your own self-imposed limitations. The effort that you exert against those obstacles transforms your soul. In this way, you grow as an individual and move further toward a life of invariable bliss.

Like white-water rafting, the principle is to enter the rapids—not avoid them. Things come to you in order to help you mature and move toward your destiny. If you rise to meet the challenge and develop from it, then the need for that situation ends and the circumstances change.

As I've discussed throughout the book, the best way to move beyond this hassle of judging events that occur in your life is to develop your sadhana, which helps you build up what yogis call a "neutral mind." You see, we all have three minds: a positive one, a negative one, and a neutral one. The positive mind tells you that everything is great, while the negative tells you that it's all bad. The neutral mind, brought to consciousness and strengthened through regular meditation, helps you see things as they are, unencumbered by emotional overlay. It helps you avoid the commotion, clash, and controversies of everyday life—in other words, you don't create karma for yourself (see Chapter 5).

When you develop your neutral mind, a peaceful state of deep, profound calm pervades your being. That isn't to say that you become flat or nonresponsive, since your sensitivity is actually enhanced. It's the capacity to recover from stresses and strains that's sharpened, so that you maintain balance in your life—and that's a living bliss.

Love, Love, Love

Maydelle is an artist in the healing group I lead. Like many people, she's had her share of difficulties and losses in life: As a young woman in the 1950s, she developed a rare case of thyroid cancer that was treated with a harsh form of radiation therapy—which caused a number of skin cancers that required surgery over the years.

Having always been what she describes as "a seeker and a helper," Maydelle now pursues renewed meaning in her life by being a kinder and more caring person. The love she feels now is different from any she's ever experienced because it comes from a new and deeper source: her soul. This has brought her a tremendous amount of life-affirming energy and palpable inner peace.

Caring this deeply means that you're truly present in the moment, often for the very first time. Yet one of the greatest tragedies of modern living is that so many people don't discover this until they're gravely ill or dying. My prayer is that *you* won't have to wait another moment to find your bliss.

Love is a miraculous force more potent than the information superhighway, gravity, or a guided missile. I don't mean romantic or familial love or companionship—I'm talking about what the ancient Greeks called "agape," or *unlimited love.* Like selfless service, agape seeks only to give, expects nothing in return, and is based upon the awareness of oneness among us all—and following the fourth New Golden Rule takes you there.

Some people intuitively perceive this as the unifying cosmic principle that holds the world together—what Dante called "the love that moves the sun and all the stars."And recall what Jesus said: "Love one another." The pure, unlimited way that he and others such as the Dalai Lama; Martin Luther King, Jr.; and Mother Teresa have shared with humanity is truth personified. For at its highest level, love requires nothing in return, and is total and constant for every person—an eternal creative force recognized by all religions and spiritual paths as a blessing. As the apostle John said: "God is love and he who abides in God, God abides in him." Seeing the Divine in all is the most prevailing quality of bliss.

When you develop the capacity to experience unlimited love, you'll notice that you begin to eliminate some of the personality traits that you'd probably like to change. It can immediately reduce your impatience, unkindness, conceit, boastfulness, rudeness, envy, and possessiveness. Moreover, a loving relationship with God has a very positive effect on your mental, emotional, and physical health, as recent medical studies have proven. You see, the more that you try to be like God by radiating unlimited love, the more you become flooded by waves of this feeling from others and from the Creator—which is life affirming.

It may be difficult for you to just start loving everyone— well, then perhaps you can at least begin with the possibility of recognizing that others have a soul just as you do, and then you'll be on the right track. Trust the Universe, and let love teach you how to live.

Stories on the Path:
My Aunt Edith, Who Saw God in All

We appreciate unlimited love most vividly at the beginning and ending of life. The birth of a baby after nine months of waiting or the death of a loved one you knew your whole life heightens your senses, and you may even approach an altered state of consciousness. I was right there when my two children were born, for example, and I recall experiencing a phenomenal natural high.

I had another intense experience at the opposite end of life's journey with the death of my Aunt Edith, who passed away in 2004 at the age of 85. It had such a poignant effect on me because she was the last adult from the generation before mine to pass away. If you've ever had that experience, then you know what I mean: It puts your own age group in the limelight, and you realize that, like it or not, you're definitely an adult—and undeniably mortal.

Well, my aunt's death made my mortality more apparent, but I knew that my soul will never die and that my being is actually infinite. This made me even happier, because I was aware of the Heaven on Earth that I live in the here-and-now. It was reflecting on my aunt's life that made such a strong impact on me.

Aunt Edith was married to my mother's brother. She was a lovely woman who enjoyed singing and dancing, and even toward the end of her life, she was very sociable and always the life of any party. She also could have been a great salesperson, making sure that her guests took a piece of cake or pie or had a cup of coffee. Visitors always had a choice, but they definitely had to have something, even if it was just a piece of fruit.

When I was a child, we spent a lot of time at my uncle and aunt's home, so my four cousins and I grew up together like brothers and sisters. After we reached adulthood, I moved away from our home in Miami Beach to the great Southwest, and I didn't return for many years. Recently, however, my wife and I began visiting south Florida again and were enjoying the sun, the beach, and the water. It was at this time that I rekindled my relationship with that part of my family. Actually getting to know my aunt as an adult was a great surprise and source of joy. We had many far-ranging conversations, which I appreciated tremendously.

Unfortunately, about five years ago, Aunt Edith developed a rare form of slow-growing cancer, which finally got the best of her. At her funeral service, I was awed by the out-pouring of love and positive sentiment, and part of what was so powerful was the similarity of everyone's memories of a very loving person who connected with their souls, loved them, accepted them as they were, and saw God in each of them. These expressions of affection were quite inspiring to all my aunt's friends and loved ones.

As my cousins got up to speak about their mom, they each commented on how awesome she was at treating them uniquely with a special kind of love and respect, being able to relate to that distinctive spark that made each of them an individual. What I also learned that day (which I might have under-appreciated before), was that she showed that consideration to *everybody*. Aunt Edith saw the unique Godliness in all beings, and knew that it's far more impor-tant to give love than to receive it. She somehow recognized intuitively that even if the whole world loves you, you could still be unfulfilled—so she gave freely from deep with-in her being.

The tremendous respect my aunt instinctively had for others' souls drew them toward her in life, as well as in death—people just wanted to be around someone like that. Of course, there was a lot of sadness at the loss of my aunt, but there was also a feeling of love and admiration that min-gled very beautifully with the grief. Because of all this unlimited love directed toward her, my aunt's funeral was actually a celebration of her life that honored who she was: someone who saw the Divine spark of God in everyone and treated all the people in her life with love, kindness, and respect.

Meditations on the Path: We Are All One

We're all here on this planet together. We may look different, speak different languages, and have different value systems, but we're the same in many ways. Unfortunately, it's human nature to categorize others, so that rather than seeing someone as a fellow Earth traveler, many people have a tendency to view their neighbor in a particular way—black, brown, Indian, African, or Chinese. Neither a person's level of education nor their sophistication seems to make a difference; and thousands of years haven't solved this problem. We've created minorities and majorities to try to show how different we are, but we've done very little to celebrate our sameness.

We've all been born at this time and space for a purpose, and we need tolerance, patience, and courage to help us discover our place on Earth—and gaining these traits requires self-development.

Use these two meditations to help you with that process:

We Are All One: Part I

This meditation should be done in a group, followed by Part II.

- **Posture:** Sit in a comfortable meditative posture in "easy pose" (see page 47) on the floor or in a chair with your back straight.

- **Mudra:** Raise both hands to shoulder level with your elbows relaxed downward. Point your index fingers up, and curl your other fingers down with your thumbs covering them.

- **Breath:** Breathe in and out forcefully through your nose, inhaling as deeply as possible and exhaling as powerfully as you can.

- **Focus:** Close your eyes and stay calm and quiet as you fight your thoughts and "nonthoughts." Hear nothing and see nothing. Try to go to the point where you just exist and merge into the rhythm of the Universe. With the power of the breath, take out the violence that separates you from others.

- **Time:** Continue for 11 minutes.

- **To finish:** Inhale deeply and hold your breath for ten seconds. Exhale and relax.

WE ARE ALL ONE: PART I

We Are All One: Part II

This meditation should be done in a group, following Part I.

- **Posture:** Hold hands with your neighbor on each side, creating a common ring of people. Everyone's eyes are closed.

- **Breath:** Breathe long and deep through your nose.

- **Time:** Continue for three minutes.

- **To finish:** Inhale deeply through your nose. Exhale and chant the words "Sat Nam" with a long, beautiful sound. Repeat twice for a total of three times.

WE ARE ALL ONE:
PART II

Thank you for joining me on this journey through the New Golden Rules. From this moment on, let's live as if we are all one. Through this union, we may be able to bring our molecules of life together and understand our own reality of Heaven on Earth.

Enjoy your journey into wellness . . . your journey to bliss.

AFTERWORD

In God I Dwell

Up here at the Summer Solstice Yoga Camp in New Mexico, I gaze at the infinite turquoise sky. This state is called the Land of Enchantment, and I can feel the spiritual energy in the air. The sun is hot here in the mountains about an hour north of Santa Fe, and I can smell the sage, the lavender, and the pine trees as I look out upon this magnificent mountain range. I can literally see for miles and miles—all the way from the Chama River Basin in the west to the Taos Mountains and their famous ski valley to the north.

During the retreat, we live in tents for a week, and it's really pretty comfortable since there are showers, bathrooms, and other amenities of civilization to make the experience of camping in the mountains quite enjoyable. There's an industrial kitchen, which ensures that we eat well, and fortunately, we also have what's called "The Tantric Shelter" to protect us from the hot sun and occasional afternoon rainstorms. The shelter is a large open space with a concrete floor and a corrugated tin roof that can easily hold 1,500 people sitting down (and probably twice that many if we're all standing up). We enjoy delicious vegetarian meals here, as well as inspiring lectures and entertaining music.

Across the way in a large tent that houses the bazaar, people set up tables where we can buy yoga clothes, books, music, and jewelry. We can also have our tarot cards read, receive a therapeutic massage, or sign up for a very effective yogic healing technique called "Sat Nam Rasayan." Every night at the Yogi Tea Café there's live music for our listening and dancing pleasure. The Summer Solstice celebration is a lot of fun.

There's a stage at the eastern end of the shelter where Yogiji (as Yogi Bhajan is affectionately called) used to sit and teach the most powerful meditation program on the face of the earth: White Tantric Yoga. However, since the late '80s (because of health issues), the courses have been taught with the help of modern video technology, with televisions situated throughout the shelter.

Our teacher still leads via his subtle body—the part of his being that a yogi can project to places he's not geographically located. Being a true master, Yogi Bhajan is able to filter from afar the subconscious material released by the participants during this meditation course, and a facilitator now acts as his satellite antenna. She sits at the front of the crowd (more than 1,000 people at a time, here at Summer Solstice) and "beams" the energy back to him. I've participated in quite a few classes presented in the original manner, and many, many more in the new video way.

Because of his tremendous energy and charisma, it was quite an event when Yogiji taught in person. During breaks between meditations, people would come up to the stage and visit, ask for a spiritual name, or request answers to important life questions. The "in-person" exercises were very successful for taking us to the next level of our personal and spiritual development—and today they're no less effective. In fact, I think that they may be stronger because the master is using his highly refined skills to work at a distance.

Practicing White Tantric Yoga

White Tantric Yoga is an ancient and time-tested science that was created millennia ago, when people were much more aware of the laws of nature and lived in greater harmony with their spirits than we do today—and it's a very powerful exercise.

During a class in this discipline, the participants sit opposite each other in long lines, males facing females. There are usually ten total lines, five each of men and women. (At times, women may pair up with women if there aren't enough men, and very rarely a man will have another male partner.) The meditation is performed when the group attains a posture as given by the yogi, gazes into each others' eyes, and either chants along with a taped mantra or sacred song or undertakes a specified breath (sometimes the eyes are closed).

Can you imagine the incredible energy generated by more than 1,000 people meditating together? I hope that someday you have the opportunity to feel this. To picture what it will be like, think of one of your more memorable meditation experiences, maybe at a retreat or a weekend program. Now imagine that it was ten times more efficient at releasing your subconscious blocks, traumas, and insecurities. *That's* the power of White Tantric.

According to ancient yogic lore, if you're able to meditate perfectly for one minute during this exercise, it's equal to ten years of another practice. I often find it difficult to focus flawlessly the entire time, so I'm grateful for the one-minute law! Miraculously, however, at the end of a meditation (be it 31 or 62 minutes), I feel my energy shift, and I arrive at a new level of vibration that gets me in what's called the "tantric stream" for that last minute of the exercise. And let me tell you, those final seconds are like being in another world.

When I'm in that flow, I feel my entire existence expand as I become limitless. Everyone under the shelter is glowing by then. Other participants say that this experience gives them the capacity to develop a deeper understanding of themselves and their own inner mysteries. In other words, they get closer to discovering who they really are and what makes them tick.

When we have that inner experience, it helps make us more tolerant and merciful, and this deeply relaxed state lets us fully express our capacity for love, creativity, and freedom. During these times, I'm able to feel the unity within everyone and experience the love that lies within the entirety of creation. My favorite part is that even though it's a demanding experience, I feel like my best self after completing a White Tantric Yoga course.

Enlightenment Becomes Me

At Summer Solstice, the White Tantric course is three days long on that sacred land at an altitude of around 7,500 feet. This year, I arrived ready to breathe clean air, drink pure water, and work on myself with members of my sangat. As Kirti and I sat down to begin the first day's activities, I had no idea that this year's retreat would so impact my life. I was about to be transformed again.

The exercises on the opening day were spiritually penetrating. They weren't all that physically demanding—we didn't have to hold our arms up in the air for an hour, for example—but they were very profound.

If you meditate regularly, you're well aware of the fact that while you may expect your mind to slow down during the process, the opposite usually happens. I call it "a thousand thoughts in the wink of an eye," as your mind tells you things such as: *I wish I'd gone to the bathroom,* or *I hope we get that mortgage,* or *Where's Jeff—he was supposed to be here,* and so on. Or sometimes your thoughts can be more profound as you explore the inner workings of your mind, but they still distract you from your purpose.

The key idea is to release the thoughts and favor your breath, mantra, or other focus of concentration. I call this attitude "starting all over again," and it's the most important aspect of meditation. In other words, when you realize that you're no longer engaged with the sound, for example, you simply refocus your attention. It's easy once you understand how to do it.

As we progressed in our tantric exercise that day with a long deep-breathing meditation while listening to a lovely healing mantra, I recognized that some very strange thoughts were going through my head—and that I wasn't too thrilled about it. Even though I kept starting all over again to focus on my breath, these thoughts remained in the forefront of my mind. I was unnerved because they were the same concerns that I'd dealt with many times before, and I thought I'd moved beyond them. There I was—someone who'd meditated for years and gone through so much spiritual growth—revisiting neurotic reminiscences of bygone relationships, jobs, and decisions.

My thoughts went something like this: *What would have happened if I'd been with her instead of her? What would have happened if I'd done this instead of that? Where would I be now if such and such had transpired?* Following this speculation, I saw a horizontal line in my consciousness. On top of it was the land of all my mental illusion—but what was on the other side? It was clear to me at that moment that I'd never broken through this floor of awareness to discover the other side of my mind, and my main questions were: *Where's the timelessness of my reality? What's on the other side of this line?*

At the end of that first day, I was shell-shocked, disappointed, and a bit frustrated. This wasn't supposed to be happening! I'd just planned to cruise along having fun at the retreat, but I went to sleep that night with a vague feeling of suspense.

I awoke the next day in an expectant mood. For some reason, my wife and I found ourselves moving very slowly, and we were late for class, arriving just in time to begin the second exercise. As we started, our eyes were open, and we chanted an affirmation—first the men and then the women—for one hour. After some time (I don't know how long exactly), I was guided to that line between realities that I'd seen the day before. On one side were my neuroses, cares, and woes . . . but what was beneath it all? I knew that I was close to discovering the answer.

Then, gently and almost imperceptibly, I was on the other side of my mind. My worldly perceptions were gone, and in their place I found God's love and blessings. I experienced and felt a new reality as I realized that so many of the things that I create drama, trauma, and commotion over are, in actuality, a substitute for dwelling in the space and energy of my Higher Power. This was an answer to my prayers.

I understood that the more we try to be like God by radiating unlimited love, the more we become flooded by waves of love from others and from the Creator—and that there's no better way to a peaceful, happy, healthy, and successful life. As I said in the Introduction: "We've been given the great gift of a body, mind, and soul." The idea isn't to be perfect, but to live in balance in order to bring peace to every aspect of our being—that's where Heaven begins.

As humans, we must deal with the mundane aspects of life, of course, but we can do so with our thoughts still in the Heavens. Bliss is remembering God with every breath; it's simply having experiences and realizing that beneath it all we're loved and blessed every single moment of our lives. And peace arrives with the revelation that God is in us—and most important, *we're also a part of God.*

Bliss can't be attained just by thinking about it—you have to work at *experiencing* it. As you know, we all have our own healing journey and spiritual path. Mine may not be exactly the same as yours, but it's my hope and prayer that *The New Golden Rules* has provided you with a framework to take the next step on the road to bliss.

What was revealed to me on the other side of my mind

takes me full circle. To enter into the Divine flow of life and live in tune with your Highest Power, a lifestyle action plan is essential. Whenever you feel overwhelmed, just keep these simple steps in mind:

1. Discover the miracle of your Divinity: Do your sadhana, serve others, and be with people who support your spiritual growth.

2. Listen attentively to the still, small voice within your soul and discover God's will for you.

3. Work to dissolve your blocks to spiritual growth—whether they be anger, grief, or fear—and become your true self.

4. See others as yourself so that you can see God in all.

Following these four simple steps will transport you to bliss, but it's definitely a process that takes time. It's like peeling off the layers of an onion: Bit by bit and piece by piece, you strip away the outer shell until you find yourself there at the core of your being, the center of your soul.

All of us are One with the infinity of Divinity, and it's faith that will take you from the darkness of materiality to the light of love. When you glimpse the Ultimate Reality within yourself, however, you no longer have to rely on faith alone, because you have experience. At that time, you enter a plane of grace where you're ceaselessly in bliss, merged with the formless energy we call God and living a life without death—in a place called Heaven on Earth.

The path may be challenging, and it may at times be slow, but progress does occur—maybe imperceptibly at first, but sometimes in a sudden flash . . . and often when you least expect it.

And in the final analysis, do you know what I learned from my meditation on that day at the Summer Solstice retreat? I confirmed that it's all about selfless service and love, which is the purpose of our existence—the basic human reality that's the ideal and the dream of every person ever born. It's the spiritual goal of life. You're so much more fulfilled when you're experiencing spiritual love than when your focus moves elsewhere.

You may think that this is impossible to attain, but I want to assure you that it isn't. By following the four New Golden Rules, you'll be led to that point where you'll be able to feel this love on a regular basis. Elusive though it may seem, it's a worthy goal to pursue.

Just remember the following:

With our love we can save the world.
With our love we can heal the planet.
It's in our hearts.
It's in our minds.
It's in our hands.
And I'm here to humbly serve you in love and bliss.

In God I dwell.
Sat Nam.

Acknowledgments

I give my deepest gratitude to my spiritual teacher, Yogi Bhajan, Master of Kundalini and White Tantric Yoga. I salute his teacher on the physical plane, Sant Hazara Singh, a direct descendant of Genghis Khan; as well as my teacher's guru on the astral plane, Guru Ram Das, known as the fourth master. (As you know from reading this book, Guru Ram Das lived in India during the 1500s and built the Golden Temple in Amritsar. He's well known for his humility and extraordinary healing power.)

It's been my daily prayer for the past few years for Guru Ram Das to grant me the shelter of his protection. I believe that he has.

About the Author

Dharma Singh Khalsa, M.D., often referred to simply as Dr. Dharma, was born in Ohio and raised in Florida. An anesthesiologist by training, he's a true leader and pioneer in the field of integrative medicine. As the President/Medical Director of the Alzheimer's Prevention Foundation International in Tucson, Arizona, Dr. Dharma was the first physician to testify before the Congress of the United States about his innovative ideas on the prevention and treatment of Alzheimer's disease.

An ordained minister and yogi, Dr. Dharma is the author of the critically acclaimed, best-selling books *Brain Longevity, The Pain Cure, Meditation as Medicine,* and *Food as Medicine.* He's also the developer of the first-ever kit to improve brain power: *The Better Memory Kit.*

Dr. Dharma has also produced a meditation CD series and pop-music album entitled *Love Is In You,* featuring his duet called *Bliss*. He lives in Tucson, Arizona, with his wife, Kirti, who's originally from Rome, Italy. He lectures and consults worldwide.

Website: **www.drdharma.com**

Resources

To learn more about Dr. Dharma's work, please visit his Website: **www.drdharma.com.** There you'll find his free newsletter, *The Healing Zone,* nutritional products, meditation CDs, DVDs, and *Love Is In You,* a pop-music CD by his group, *Bliss,* featuring Dr. D and Master L. All of the mind/body exercises in this book can be found at this Website.

Dharma Singh Khalsa, M.D.
2420 N. Pantano Rd.
Tucson, AZ 85715
Phone: (520) 749-8374
Fax: (520) 296-6640

To schedule a professional speaking engagement by Dr. Dharma, please feel free to contact Jo Cavender at Speakers Connection: **www.speakersconnection.com** • phone: (800) 697-7325, ext. 1.

To find a certified Kundalini Yoga teacher in your area, please contact the International Kundalini Yoga Teachers Association at **www.kundaliniyoga.com** • phone: (505) 367-1313.

Hay House Titles of Related Interest

*Cracking the Coconut Code:
7 Insights to Transform Your Life, by Mary Jo McCabe

The Disappearance of the Universe: *Straight Talk about
Illusions, Past Lives, Religion, Sex, Politics,
and the Miracles of Forgiveness,* by Gary R. Renard

Everything I've Ever Done That Worked, by Lesley Garner

The Gift of Peace:
Guideposts on the Road to Serenity, by Ben Stein

The Power of Intention: *Learning to Co-create Your World
Your Way,* by Dr. Wayne W. Dyer

*Practical Praying: *Using the Rosary to Enhance Your Life,*
by John Edward

Vitamins for the Soul: *Daily Doses of Wisdom for Personal
Empowerment,* by Sonia Choquette

*Published by Princess Books; distributed by Hay House

All of the above are available at your local bookstore,
or may be ordered by visiting:
Hay House USA: **www.hayhouse.com;** Hay House Australia:
www.hayhouse.com.au; Hay House UK: **www.hayhouse.co.uk;**
Hay House South Africa: **orders@psdprom.co.za**

We hope you enjoyed this Hay House book.
If you'd like to receive a free catalog featuring additional
Hay House books and products, or if you'd like information about
the Hay Foundation, please contact:

Hay House, Inc.
P.O. Box 5100
Carlsbad, CA 92018-5100

(760) 431-7695 or **(800) 654-5126**
(760) 431-6948 (fax) or **(800) 650-5115 (fax)**
www.hayhouse.com

Published and distributed in Australia by: Hay House Australia Pty.
Ltd. • 18/36 Ralph St. • Alexandria NSW 2015 • *Phone:* 612-9669-4299
• *Fax:* 612-9669-4144 • www.hayhouse.com.au

Published and distributed in the United Kingdom by: Hay House UK,
Ltd. • Unit 62, Canalot Studios • 222 Kensal Rd., London W10 5BN •
Phone: 44-20-8962-1230 • *Fax:* 44-20-8962-1239 •
www.hayhouse.co.uk

Published and distributed in the Republic of South Africa by: Hay
House SA (Pty), Ltd., P.O. Box 990, Witkoppen 2068 •
Phone/Fax: 27-11-706-6612 • orders@psdprom.co.za

Distributed in Canada by: Raincoast • 9050 Shaughnessy St.,
Vancouver, B.C. V6P 6E5 • *Phone:* (604) 323-7100 • *Fax:* (604) 323-2600

Sign up via the Hay House USA Website to receive the Hay House
online newsletter and stay informed about what's going on with your
favorite authors. You'll receive bimonthly announcements about:
Discounts and Offers, Special Events, Product Highlights, Free
Excerpts, Giveaways, and more!
www.hayhouse.com